Narcissistic Abuse

Practical Strategies to Put a Narcissist in Their Place and Break the Cycle of Emotional and Psychological Abuse

Grace Horton

©Copyright 2021 – *Grace Horton* - All rights reserved

The content contained within this book may not be reproduced, duplicated, or transmitted without direct written permission from the author or the publisher.

Under no circumstances will any blame or legal responsibility be held against the publisher, or author, for any damages, reparation, or monetary loss due to the information contained within this book, either directly or indirectly.

Legal Notice

This book is copyright protected. This book is only for personal use. You cannot amend, distribute, sell, use, quote or paraphrase any part, or the content within this book, without the consent of the author-publisher.

Disclaimer Notice

Please note the information contained within this document is for educational and entertainment purposes only. All effort has been executed to present accurate, up to date, and reliable, complete information. No warranties of any kind are declared or implied. Readers acknowledge that the author is not engaging in the rendering of legal, financial, medical, or professional advice.

Table of Contents

Introduction 4

Chapter 1 What is Narcissistic Abuse? 9

Chapter 2 How Narcissists Abuse 27

Chapter 3 Gaslighting 36

Chapter 4 Narcissist Target: Traits that Makes You a Prime Target for Narcissists 42

Chapter 5 Coping with a Narcissist 50

Chapter 6 Surviving Narcissistic Abuse 67

Chapter 7 Helping a Narcissist Recover 84

Chapter 8 The Narcissist and The Empathy 92

Chapter 9 Healing from Narcissistic Abuse 107

Chapter 10 Dating After Leaving a Narcissist 117

Chapter 11 Case Study and its Implications 124

Conclusion 132

Introduction

Narcissistic abuse is a form of abuse that is difficult to identify and heal from. Narcissists are natural born actors, and they use their special assets to manipulate their victims into believing their behavior is justified. They often come across as charismatic, likable, and charming in public, but there's another side to them that they only show behind closed doors where the true nature of their personality is revealed. According to the Merriam-Webster Dictionary, narcissistic abuse is: "The condition of suffering from chronic or repeated devaluation of self-worth by a primary caretaker, with the resulting in development of narcissistic personality traits."

While in essence this definition may be true, the root cause cannot be attributed to one person and narcissism can develop as a result of different factors that play a role in shaping personality. While some may argue that it is merely a manifestation of a personality disorder, others believe that upbringing and environment contribute to its development. It's not as simple as pointing a finger at one person and blaming him/her for the inevitable misery a victim or two may experience. At times, it's hard to detect, but if you see the signs of narcissism in any relationship, be it intimate or professional, let it be a warning that you might end up with someone who is abusive.

Table of Contents

Introduction 4

Chapter 1 What is Narcissistic Abuse? 9

Chapter 2 How Narcissists Abuse 27

Chapter 3 Gaslighting 36

Chapter 4 Narcissist Target: Traits that Makes You a Prime Target for Narcissists 42

Chapter 5 Coping with a Narcissist 50

Chapter 6 Surviving Narcissistic Abuse 67

Chapter 7 Helping a Narcissist Recover 84

Chapter 8 The Narcissist and The Empathy 92

Chapter 9 Healing from Narcissistic Abuse 107

Chapter 10 Dating After Leaving a Narcissist 117

Chapter 11 Case Study and its Implications 124

Conclusion 132

Introduction

Narcissistic abuse is a form of abuse that is difficult to identify and heal from. Narcissists are natural born actors, and they use their special assets to manipulate their victims into believing their behavior is justified. They often come across as charismatic, likable, and charming in public, but there's another side to them that they only show behind closed doors where the true nature of their personality is revealed. According to the Merriam-Webster Dictionary, narcissistic abuse is: "The condition of suffering from chronic or repeated devaluation of self-worth by a primary caretaker, with the resulting in development of narcissistic personality traits."

While in essence this definition may be true, the root cause cannot be attributed to one person and narcissism can develop as a result of different factors that play a role in shaping personality. While some may argue that it is merely a manifestation of a personality disorder, others believe that upbringing and environment contribute to its development. It's not as simple as pointing a finger at one person and blaming him/her for the inevitable misery a victim or two may experience. At times, it's hard to detect, but if you see the signs of narcissism in any relationship, be it intimate or professional, let it be a warning that you might end up with someone who is abusive.

In current society, everyone easily comes across a narcissist. The internet has given us an easy way to seek out potential partners that we might not have otherwise found. Some people fall into bad relationships because they are not aware of the traits of a narcissist. This can be dangerous because a narcissistic can easily spot a potential victim and manipulate him/her by taking advantage of the fact that he/she might relate to them. The first sign that you might be in an abusive relationship is when your partner is always trying to get all the attention. When you don't pay any attention to him/her, they will use different strategies like creating drama or whatever it takes so you focus on them. A narcissist may be very jealous, controlling, and manipulative in an unhealthy manner.

A healthy relationship is one where both partners are well adjusted in a balanced manner. But when we start to recognize the signs of narcissistic behavior, it becomes easy to identify narcissistic traits. The signs to be aware of are:

1. Your partner is always trying to get your attention. This can be done through constant texting, calling you all the time, and even sending unwanted gifts that you don't need or want but are too polite or considerate to refuse.
2. Your partner has an over-inflated ego and characterizes himself/herself as a person who is intelligent and superior to most people in the world.

3. Your partner does not treat his/her victim with basic human respect and dignity. For example, if your partner insults you, he/she will never consider apologizing or making amends.
4. Your partner is condescending and superior in public but becomes very polite when alone with you.

In terms of relationships, narcissists thrive on control; they find it difficult to comprehend or accept that their victims have a definite opinion about certain issues. Therefore, it's normal that the victims be commanded to do certain things without being given any reason or explanation. They'll usually make abusive statements like, "When I shout you will do what I want," or "If you don't fall in line, nobody will love you." Narcissists tend to be possessive in relationships which can cause a lot of tension as they always think there's someone else whose attention is better than theirs.

One of the biggest issues people have with narcissism is that they feel as though they are being controlled by their partner rather than the other way round. While many might not see it as abuse, others would argue that while there is an element of control in most relationships, it shouldn't come across as abusive. While many people have the ability to be manipulative and controlling, it's the way that they go about it that is the biggest sign. This book will show you how not to get trapped in a relationship with a narcissist.

Narcissist is a word we come across almost every day, but what does it mean? In this book, we explored every point of it, and every angle was well researched to give you the best and well-compiled research on the subject. You may be struggling in your relationship, at home or with your friend and feel you are never enough. No matter how much you give it your best, you never really satisfy them, and you never reach the point they want you to. You feel like whatever you do is never good enough for them.

Well, this is the right book for you. You identify some characteristics of the typical narcissist, and now you will be able to understand the behaviors of some people and get to know why they do what they do. You may learn to accept the fact that you are not always the problem, but they are. Going deeper into this, you will know better how to handle such people. It might have been hard dealing with someone who demeans you all the time, is not able to understand you or even care what you are feeling.

You will know how to deal with a narcissist and live with them under the same roof without trying to please them. As wise man once said that at times, it is good to be a coward. When it comes a narcissist, you are actually not dealing with them at all, and you need to avoid these people at all costs. It's better to stick with others. We will give you some tips on how to prevent narcissist from entering your life or when you identify one, you know to run for your dear life before it is too late.

A narcissist can drain you and kill your self-esteem. to save yourself, stay away from them: that is the only way out. This will be a life-changing experience.

Chapter 1
What is Narcissistic Abuse?

Narcissists don't love themselves; they are driven by shame. It is an idealized picture they use to convince themselves that they embody what they admire. But deep down, a narcissistic feels a gap between the facade shown to the world and their ego-based shame. They work hard to prevent shame. This gap also applies to other offenders, but the narcissist uses defensive mechanisms that destroy normal conditions and cause pain and damage to the confidence of his loved ones. (To diagnose a narcissistic personality disorder, use "NPD").

Many narcissistic coping mechanisms are offensive; hence, the term "narcissistic abuse". However, someone can be abusive and not be a narcissist. Addicts and people with other mental disorders, such as bipolar disorder, antisocial personality disorder (sociopathy), and cross-border personality disorder are also abusive. Abuse is abuse, regardless of the diagnosis. If you're a victim of abuse, the biggest challenges are:

- Clear identification

- Building a support system

- Learn how to protect oneself

Abuse can be mental, physical, financial, spiritual or sexual. Here are some examples of abuse that you might not have detected:

Verbal violence: includes degradation, bullying, accusation, accusation, accusation, shame, demanding, orderly, threatening, criticizing, sarcasm, furious, averted, undermining, disrupting, blocking, and abusive. Note that many people sometimes use sarcasm, interrupt you, resist, criticize, blame or block. Consider the context, anger, and frequency of behavior before calling it narcissistic abuse.

Manipulation: generally affects someone who support self-centered and motivated goals. It often expresses a hidden aggression. Think of the "wolf in sheep's clothing". At first glance, the words appear harmless and they even complement each other; but underneath you feel humiliated or hostile. If your manipulation is entrenched, you may not recognize it as such.

Emotional extortion: include threats, anger, warnings, threats or punishment. It is a form of manipulation that casts doubt upon you. You feel a fear, duty and/or guilt, sometimes referred to as "FOG."

Gas Lighting: intentionally causes your suspicions to support your negative perception of reality or the belief that you are mentally incompetent.

Competition: competitive is high and insidious with a narcissist, sometimes with the use of unethical means. For example, cheating in a game.

Negative contrast: compare and contrasting you with narcissists or other people.

Sabotage: interfering with your efforts or relationships for revenge or personal gain.

Usage and objectification: using you for personal purposes regardless of your feelings or needs.

Recumbent: persistent scams without accountability or achieving the narcissist's goals.

Choice: things like money, sex, communication or love.

Ignoring : ignore the needs of a child for which the offender is responsible. Includes endangering children such as leaving a child in a potentially harmful situation.

Invasion of privacy: ignoring your personal borders by tracking you by phone or email; denying your physical privacy, chasing or follow you; ignoring the privacy you desire.

<u>Character defamation</u>: Spreading harmful gossip or lies about you to others.

<u>Violence</u>: blocking your movements, pulling you, throwing things, or destroying your property.

<u>Financial abuse</u>: includes controlling financial domination or emptying your finances by blackmailing, stealing, manipulating or gambling, or even creating debt in your name or selling your personal property.

<u>Isolation:</u> isolate you from friends, family, or access to external services and support through control, manipulation, verbal abuse, assassination, or other forms of abuse.

Malignant Narcissism and Sociopathy

A person with excessive narcissistic qualities who behaves harmfully and hostilely is considered to have "harmful narcissism". Harmful narcissists do not suffer guilt. They can be sadistic and enjoy causing pain. They can be so competitive and unprincipled that they exhibit anti-social behavior. Paranoia places them in a defensive attack mode as a means of self-defense.

Malignant narcissism is akin to sociopathy. Sociopaths have been crushed or damaged in some way so they exhibit narcissistic traits; but not all narcissists are sociopathic. Their motivations are different. While narcissists are ideal persons to be admired, sociopaths reach only for their self-sufficient agenda. They have to win at all costs and do not think about violating social norms and laws. They don't care about people like narcissists do.

Narcissists do not want to be abandoned. They depend on the approval of others, but sociopaths easily release relationships that do not serve them. Although some narcissists think about achieving their goals, they are usually more reactive than sociopaths who figure out their cold and evil plans.

You may have asked yourself at least a thousand times, "Why am I staying in this madness?" You may have come up with a possible answer - the fear of being alone - while acknowledging that your experience is not necessarily real fear itself. By assessing why you have remained in such an emotionally destructive relationship, you might conclude that although you prefer company; you also realize that discomfort and emotional pain come with the narcissist in your life.

You realize that you would be lonely by giving up this reality, and you distance yourself from grief to survive. You can experience, at least temporarily, some relief from emotional pain and discomfort. Yet it is unlike the emotional pain experienced by the narcissist who as an emotional addict and despite your efforts to attract their attention through various activities gets no relief.

You've found that you can be in the midst of your beloved family and friends, attend a long-awaited concert at a professional sporting event, go to a beautiful beach with perfect weather, yet have a broken heart. Unfortunately, you are unique in this experience. People advise, "Life continues. Come on. Stop apologizing. Don't give this person time to think about them. They certainly don't think about you." If all the well-meaning outsiders just knew how hard you have tried! Why are you going into this world of fear? Have you been told, "You must love pain because you are the one who chooses to stay with a narcissistic emotional addict?" It doesn't make sense to others, nor does it make sense to you.

You keep asking why? That's a good thing because only you can find the answer. Your journey is so unique. Will this curse ever be a blessing? If you survive, yes it will. The struggle, if you're still involved with a narcissistic emotional addict, is whether you want to survive. This does not mean that you are going to die, but it is also a possibility. What is being said here is that you existed before crossing paths with a narcissistic emotional abuser. You used to laugh, create, jump and run, smile and enjoy simple things in life. After joining a narcissistic r emotions, the colors, sounds, and smells of life have been lost to you. You live and breathe but feel dead inside, except for the pain stomach pain. Nothing makes more sense. You ask again, Why do I stay in this chaos? Why do I love them so much? Why do I love them more than my own life? Why? There is the possible joy of the "golden egg". Maybe they promises you to travel, own a house or build a bigger, nicer house. Do they have a lot of money? Does it make you feel like no friend has given you any similar feeling? When you are in their presence, no one else matters.

Think about it. What do they have on you? It's like a curse with an invisible power. You feel the curse attracting the narcissistic emotional abuser. It is like being in a prison cell with the door open, but you can't walk and stay outside. What kind of golden egg do they have? What did they do to make you start to believe that you can't live without them? They may deny this reality, even if you have clear evidence to support your case. Do you think somewhere in your mind that you are the winner of a revered golden goose if they choose you instead of all others?

Finding and understanding the golden egg with the narcissistic emotional culprit can be a challenge. Discovering your golden egg will reveal your most important uncertainties. This fear is so great in you that you risk death. You choose to endure abuse instead of dealing with it and making it become too real. It is said that most people die with the music that is still there. Do you have the courage to be yourself?

If you seek and find the golden egg with a narcissistic emotional abuser in your life, your curse will become a blessing. Be encouraged and dare to be you.

TYPES OF NARCISSISTS

Full-Blown Narcissist

A full-blown narcissist is the type that is not predictable nor preventable. These are types of people who strike when it is least expected, and nothing can be done to stop them. This is mainly characterized by an arrogance that disrupts and blows things out of proportion. Full-blown narcissism is the last stage where all the characteristics of narcissism have been blended and the victim, most of the time, turns out to be violent and uncontrollable. They can throw things everywhere or even mess because of a pure provocation at anything you do; a full-blown narcissist will always find a reason to get mad.

Covert Narcissist

A covert narcissist is the inverse of the overt narcissist in that they crave and demand self-importance and admiration, unlike the overt type who always needs to be right. Covert narcissistic behaviors are soft and subtle. Although they crave fame and recognition, they do it in ways that do not infringe another person's rights. The only difference between a covert and a full-blown narcissist is that the former chooses not to outwardly manifest their longing while the latter are fully intent on letting their demands known. In other words, coverts are an introverted version of full-blown narcissists although both fantasize about their self-worthiness and self-importance; the only difference is the way they manifest them. Many people have fallen victim of a covert narcissist because of the insidious way they work; you will never understand the harm they bring on their victims until much of it has been witnessed.

The primary characteristic of the overt narcissist is passive self-importance. They don't inflate their quest and thirst for admiration and importance, and they get them anyhow. Another trait of the covert narcissist is shaming others. Coverts never want to carry the blame, and they would rather shame and blame others for elevating themselves to be seen as of a higher caliber.

People With Narcissistic Tendencies

There are people who are narcissists, and there are people who are not narcissists but have narcissistic tendencies. One can manifest the traits of narcissists without being one. For instance, they can be self-centered with low empathy, and still they are not narcissists. So what qualifies one to be a narcissist, and what differentiates people with narcissistic traits from true narcissists?

People with narcissistic tendencies divide the populace into two: those to be looked up to and those to be looked down on. Unlike narcissists, people with narcissistic tendencies are realistic but instead have qualities worth emulating and others that are worth nothing.

The primary traits of people with narcissistic tendencies are domineering and always appear to know it all, but they will not be battling with self-esteem issues that the narcissists are fighting and grappling with. The only difference between the narcissists and people with narcissistic tendencies is that the people with tendencies have the capacity to see people as a mixture of good and evil and be able to associate themselves with the good ones while having nothing to do with the bad ones.

Narcissistic abuse is not exclusive. This kind of physical torment has happened to millions of people in the world. If it has happened to you too or is already happening to you now, know that you are not alone. You may be asking yourself, "Why me?" You might be feeling that this woeful experience is only happening to you. You might even blame yourself and feel like you are not good enough. But the truth is, you are not alone, and it is not your fault.

If you can, research about the experience you have been going through. Check on the internet about it. Take the next step and reach out for help. Talk to trusted people like professional counselors, experienced therapists, psychologists, friends, and family members that you can trust. You can even contact trauma facilities. Your healing will start immediately. You begin to see the reality of what has been happening to you. Seek help soon, especially if you are experiencing extreme symptoms like suicidal thoughts.

Make safety plans if you begin to see signs of people close to you becoming violent. In an abusive relationship, a trauma bond develops between the abuser and the abused. This is due to the hopelessness instilled in the abused person. However, sometimes moving and finding safety is less expensive than staying and taking in more abuse. It is possible to reach a point of recovery, with no or limited contact with the victim. The road to recovery is not easy, but it is worth it. The final destination will be attaining your freedom and getting yourself back on your feet.

In a nutshell, this is how narcissist abuse looks like: your happiness is denied, you lose your self-identity and have no freedom of expression. You are only there to listen and not to talk. You are to be seen not to heard. Your reality is warped and distorted. You are abused, threatened, manipulated, lied to, ridiculed, and taken through some ugly experiences. Then you are made to believe that you imagine things. You are called "mad" and told that you only have yourself to blame.

Perhaps you were even replaced and thrown out. Then you were lured back into the same cycle of abuse, this time with more painful experiences. You are stalked, harassed, and made to stay with the abuser by force. The most painful part is that the person doing all this to you is the very person who is supposed to protect you from it. It is the person you trusted and had hope in.

These are not the ups and downs of a healthy relationship no matter how much you might want to convince yourself that your companion is unique. This is an abusive companion who will break your soul, kill your sense of self, or even worse, your physical being. Other people will not understand, for you may not have physical scars to show. All you have are the internal wounds, fractured memories, and mental battles. This sounds very horrific. But don't be scared as it is possible to get yourself together. You can get your life back.

GETTING YOURSELF TOGETHER

Here are tips that will help you get yourself together.

Game Changing

Narcissists sabotage their victim's minds. They will make you believe that all that should matter to you is doing what they want without a second thought. Forget yourself and start singing songs of adoration to them. Sadly, no matter how much you give yourself to them, they are never satisfied. They get you on your toes at every moment. You keep thinking which of the next demands you should meet. Eventually, you bend to their desires. Don't get too involved in the narcissist monopoly conversations about what you have done wrong. Give yourself a break. tell yourself that it is not true. Detach fast and don't swallow that verbal poison.

Misrepresenting Your Thoughts and Words

Toxic narcissists perceive themselves as mind readers. They think they know what other people are thinking. They say things like, "I know you, I know what you want to say, I know how you think." They will put words into your mouth. They complete your sentences even before they begin. Also, before you get a chance to call out their misbehavior, they already are ready with excuses. You can only think about what they want you to believe, and you can only say what they want you to say. This is not good of course. The narcissist never evaluates what is really happening because they can't and won't come into terms with reality. They react to their triggers, created in their world of delusions.

State your case firmly and walk away with no more arguments. Do not give them a chance to shift the blame to you. The more you entrain them, the more they convince you that you should be ashamed of accusing them, and this could give them more rights to future abuse.

Changing the Subject

This is their common tactic. A narcissist will never want to be held accountable for any misdeed. They always redirect the conversation. The redirection often lands on one of the mistakes of the accuser. Narcissists are never afraid of pulling out your past mistakes, even if it committed ten years ago. They make it look so bad and render their accusers powerless by holding them accountable for everything. When this diversion happens, redirect it back to the original topic. State firmly that is not what you wanted to discuss. If they still insist on blaming you, stop the conversation and keep yourself busy with something else.

Smearing

A narcissist is capable of abusing deliberately so that you will react, and then they will use your reactions against you. They slander you and report back to anybody who cares to listen. They create stories to show that you are the abuser and they are the victim. Ironically, they accuse you of doing the wrong things they themselves do as a cover-up not to get the blame.

When this happens, seek help and avoid confrontation with the abuser. They will provoke and hurt you until you can't take it anymore. Then, they watch and wait for your reactions, which they will use against you. In case you seek justice, it is good to talk to a lawyer familiar with Narcissist Personality Disorder.

Triangulating

The narcissist may bring the views and opinions of other people into the dynamics of the relationship to validate their harmful actions and invalidate the reactions of their significant other. They triangulate them to parents, siblings, coworkers, strangers, and everyone else that matters. Triangulation can include love triangles. This influence other partners to use their opinions against you. This leaves you hanging, feeling insecure, and full of self-doubt. This is a tactic to disorient you from the toxic narcissist's behavior. It leads you to believe in their self-perception that they are desirable and perfect people. The narcissist also likes to report false information of what others say about you. This leaves you questioning yourself and feeling terrible about who you are.

To overcome triangulation, try your best to seek your validation. You can also reverse-triangulate a narcissist by gaining support from another person who is not influenced by the narcissist. The third party the narcissist is triangulating with is also triangulating with you. You are being played all around.

Preemptive Defense

A toxic narcissist likes to give themselves endless praise that has no basis. Despite having very dysfunctional behaviors, they want to show themselves up as a nice guy. Their conversations are full of boastful statements about how good they are and how other people should be associated with them. They overestimate their ability to be compassionate and kind.

These abusers expect everyone to see them as they see themselves. They cannot stand anybody who sees them as anything less than the right person. That is why their affinity for praise and affirmation never ends. They tell people to trust them even when they have not built a foundation for trust. Their false mask slips off as the abuse gets full brown and the cold and contemptuous personality is revealed. The victim becomes frustrated.

Your preemptive defense can be countered, so focus not on what the narcissist says, but what they do. Investigate why they insist on being a good person. You will find it is because they know you should not trust them, and they are afraid you will get to know this.

Sugarcoating

Malicious people find it fun to mess with others. They test and tease other people's mind then make it a joke. As discussed, narcissists are capable of squeezing your insecurities out of you, then document and use it in the future. They tell you something harmful to measure your reaction. They say they did not mean it and pretend to be innocent. This leaves you confused and vulnerable to future attacks. At this stage, you are being baited to stop being defensive altogether.

Your instincts can tell you when there are baiting and sugar coating. When they say something wrong and then ask you to take it lightly, that is a red flag. Do not listen to false flattery. Internalize what you feel about it and leave some space for detaching.

Being under the narcissist's manipulation is no joke. It is better to know how to counter them as early as possible. If you are already in it, take the first step. Be bold and seek all the help you can. If legal advice is required, do not hesitate to get it.

Chapter 2
How Narcissists Abuse

Many people are unaware of the abuse they suffer from a narcissist or just don't know that what they're going through is abuse because narcissistic abuse can be difficult to identify. Narcissistic behavior goes beyond being simply selfish and egocentric; it crosses into manipulation and brainwashing where the victim loses all sense of self-worth and independence.

Narcissists often spend time charming their victims while simultaneously criticizing them in private. They get you to invest your energy, emotions, and money in them then discard you without remorse when the relationship ends. It's a form of mental and emotional abuse that can leave the victim feeling confused, exhausted, and stressed. They may develop into Post-Traumatic Stress Disorder (PTSD) where depression, flashbacks and anxiety are not uncommon.

When someone is victimized by a narcissist for any length of time, it creates long-term effects on that person's life. The victim will have to suffer from the aftermath of narcissistic abuse for years after the relationship is over. They might spend years trying to make sense of what happened in their relationship with the narcissist, trying to understand how someone they loved so much could treat them so horrendously. They might have to bury their feelings deep inside so as not upset other people around them. They might have low self-esteem, feel worthless or guilty, and blame themselves for the narcissist's abusive behavior.

It's normal for someone who suffered from narcissistic abuse to be confused and conflicted because they often idealized their abuser in the beginning of the relationship. They are reluctant to admit that the person they idolized is actually a dangerous abuser who has now completely shattered their self-esteem. Many victims think that they will be blamed by others when they start talking about how they were abused by a narcissist, so they keep quiet.

The following are ways in which narcissists abuse people:

Extreme Jealousy

The narcissist has an inverse sense of sexuality where they constantly feel inferior and jealous because they need constant admiration and attention to feed their fragile ego. They will often exhibit extreme paranoia about their partner's feelings for others, even if they have absolutely no reason to doubt them. If you are in a relationship with a narcissist, or had one in the past, then you probably remember countless late night fights because they got jealous over someone just trying to be friendly.

Using Guilt and Emotional Blackmail

The narcissist will use guilt, threats, and emotional blackmail to get what they want. The narcissist will accuse you of doing things that you probably didn't do (even though you wouldn't have done it if they hadn't asked). Narcissists know how to manipulate people by using fear and threats. They will also use guilt. You might have done something wrong in the narcissist's eyes, but they won't say anything directly; instead, they just accuse you of being a bad person and trying to escape them.

When you're in a relationship with a narcissist, you will often feel guilty like you're in the wrong. You might be feeling guilty about something they accused you of doing that you didn't do, or it could just be the way they accuse you of what is happening that makes you feel bad.

You might feel as though it was your fault for some reason, but the narcissist is the one who acted like a sociopathic child and has completely destroyed their partner's self-esteem. they continue to do so by assailing their partner with narcissistic rage. It's only normal to feel stressed when going through narcissistic abuse because it involves multiple forms of abuse all at once.

You may feel like everything you do is wrong, that you're a horrible person, and no one else would want to be with you. These are all normal feelings after being abused by a narcissist. The narcissist will do anything they can to make you feel guilty because it makes it easier for them to control you and keep you in the relationship.

Degradation and Humiliation

When you're in a relationship with a narcissist, you will feel small and worthless. You might even feel like you don't exist or your needs are unimportant. The narcissist will do anything to make sure that they feel superior to you in every way. They may constantly put you down or humiliate you in private by making jokes at your expense or by making fun of the things important to you.

Abusive Comments and Verbal Abuse

The narcissist won't say anything directly when they want to get their point across. It's all indirect, subtle, and oftentimes disguised as a joke or by making fun of you. If you start saying something, the narcissist might laugh at you because they know that will make you feel bad, and it makes it easier for them to control you.

The narcissist will find a way to make your life difficult without directly admitting it. They will use passive aggressive comments when they want to say something directly to piss you off without giving anything up in return. They have learned to never say anything in plain sight unless they want other people to know that they are being abusive towards their partner.

This also creates fear in the victim. They often cannot tell if they are being abused because they are so afraid of the consequences of it not working out. This is more common in people who haven't been abused before. Many times this abuse will come in the form of passive aggressive remarks or emotional abuse which can be harder to spot and prove.

Projection and Accusations

The narcissist will accuse you of things without actually saying anything directly to you. Of course, they will usually accuse you of doing things you probably didn't do, but it is equally likely they did do so as a way for them to exert control over your life.

Projective Identification and Provoking Defensiveness

The narcissist may start to make comments that are strange without really saying anything. They may accuse you of being a certain way or having certain traits that they actually have themselves. This is very common with abusive narcissistic relationships because the narcissist often has an extreme form of insecurity and feels that they need to prove their worth by destroying the other person instead of building a stronger relationship as a reciprocal exchange.

Engulfing, Entitlement, and Abusive Dependency

In this relationship dynamic, the narcissist will become so entwined in your life that it becomes difficult to live your own life. They will check up on you constantly and become the center of your life. They will oftentimes not leave you alone unless they think you are cheating on them or something else is wrong in your life.

They rarely give you your space. The narcissist wants to control what you do, who you are with, and what kind of friends you have. Even if it's not really that bad in their minds, they will often try to manipulate situations or people so it feels like everything is falling apart around them without actually doing anything bad themselves to make it happen.

Unreasonable Expectations of Reciprocity and Unpredictability

The narcissist is extremely unpredictable. They are very likely to do or say something that doesn't make any sense. They may give you gifts and be extremely kind and then turn around and talk about how much they hate you. This is because they feel entitled to have something when they want it, regardless of the fact that other people in their environment also exist on the same planet.

They will give you their attention when it suits them and then ignore you for days. They will demand a lot from their partners but not really give much in return. They will expect you to be on call for them 24/7 and have no problem making you feel like your life revolves around them.

Excessive Need for Admiration

Narcissists demand a lot of admiration and attention. They have a big "I'm the center of attention" mindset that can make it very difficult for their partners to get any attention or love from the other people in their lives. This means that they will likely become jealous if you friends, and they are not included in these relationships. They will get angry and upset if you take time doing things that don't involve them. That's a deal breaker for me.

And finally, the one thing that gets to me is when they talk bad about others behind their backs. Then I get really mad and upset. This is like cutting off your nose to spite your face. It's so stupid and shows a lack of respect. It is totally selfish and inconsiderate. Don't do it!

If you are married or in a committed relationship, only talk to your partner and other people in confidence or with full disclosure…it kills a friendship real fast when the person you are talking about finds out that you were talking behind their back.

When someone is narcissistic, it's easy to get sucked in. It seem like they are the only person you can count on. They will be very charming and personable with you in the beginning of the relationship because they want to seem like a person who values your friendship and interest.

This is usually when you become the victim of their manipulation and abuse. It might even take years for the full extent of it to hit home. It is very likely that you'll wake up one day and realize that you were deceived. You might be afraid to confront them because they are usually very good at making you feel guilty and that it's your fault you were abused.

The narcissist will use your emotions and heart against you. They will say things that make it seem like they care about you when they are actually just trying to get more control over your life to get what they want. If you are dating a narcissist, you need to walk away before they destroy your life. They will eat their way through your self-esteem and make sure that you never trust another person again.

Narcissistic abuse is extremely dangerous, and it is wise to walk away from the relationship. The forces of narcissism are scary, and if you let them get a hold of you, they will destroy your life. Your self-esteem won't be the only thing they will take. Chances are, they'll also destroy your sanity and self-worth. Please don't make the same mistakes I did and don't let a narcissist continue to abuse you.

Chapter 3
Gaslighting

Narcissists are absolute masters of manipulation. They can turn your whole life upside down in the blink of an eye. Unfortunately, what people don't often realize is that this abuse doesn't end there; it can continue for years after the relationship is over. This chapter will examine a common form of abuse from narcissists called gaslighting, which causes victims to second guess themselves and their perceptions.

Gaslighting is a form of emotional abuse where manipulators get in your head and convince you that what you know and see with your own eyes isn't real; it's all just happening in your head. This type of abuse is so effective because it happens gradually over time, making it very hard to notice that you're being manipulated.

What Does Gaslighting Look Like?

Gaslighting abuse manipulates memories, thoughts and emotions. It happens when someone says something that isn't true as if it is, but you are so confused that you begin second-guessing yourself. One common tactic the narcissist uses to gaslight his victims is called "blanking" the victim. This means that at certain points, the narcissist will try to erase a person from their memory or pretend like they never existed; this includes pretending like certain events or conversations never happened. This type of gaslighting can be especially damaging because the narcissist is essentially denying his partner's reality.

Gaslighting also includes twisting a victim's perception of their own reality. One obvious form is lying to someone, but it can be much more subtle than that. Let's say both David and Brandi are at home in their apartment when Jane, who they know, comes to the door to drop something off as she often does.

In this situation, Brandi has answered the door and is startled to see Jane there; she thought she was alone with David who is reading. Now Jane walks in and sees David reading a book instead of being on his computer as he usually is at this time of the day. Jane questions David and asks him what he is doing. David says he was doing some research for work, which is true. However, Brandi heard this and thought to herself, Really? He's telling Jane that he was doing research for work when he said only thirty minutes ago he said that he was going to take a break from the computer to read? This is where things get tricky. Brandi continues to have doubts about David's claims even though they were all true.

The most extreme form of gaslighting can potentially cause the victim to start questioning their own sanity, making them think that they themselves are crazy. Gaslighting is one of the most toxic forms of emotional abuse because it so completely infects your reality. It takes a lot of strength to stand up to this type of manipulation because you have to convince yourself that what you know and see with your own two eyes really happened. If you begin to doubt yourself, it makes it easier for the manipulator to get away with his or her abuse.

How Does Gaslighting Happen?

Gaslighting abuse isn't just a one-time occurrence; it happens over an extended period of time and gives the abuser the chance to manipulate his or her victim over and over again. It starts by slowly gaining trust to access the partner's life. Once she has gained access, she begins to slowly confuse and manipulate the victim over time. The gaslighting abuser changes their stories, contradicts themselves, and twists reality to make it sound like the victim is delusional.

The abuser also starts other arguments to deflect attention away from their own lies. At this point, the victim begins to have doubts about themselves and what they believe is real, which causes them to question their own reality. The manipulator then uses these doubts against the victim while continuing the abuse.

How to Deal with Gaslighting

There are three main ways to deal with gaslighting. The first is not to be controlled by it because when you are gaslighted, you are essentially being controlled by the abuser. You are not in control of yourself, making it extremely difficult to escape the situation. The second way is to learn how to recognize the signs and tell people what's going on. This will make it easier for your friends and family members see what is happening. The third way is to have a support system in place while confronting your abuser; it's hard enough to deal with an abusive relationship without support from those around you.

How to Deal with Your Own Doubts

In every abusive situation, the victim becomes the person they're trying to escape. They lose their identity, and they don't know themselves anymore. This is why it's so important to take time for yourself to get back in touch with who you really are. Don't let someone else define you - it's your life. Take some time for yourself and reflect on what you want and need out of life; this will help you rediscover parts of yourself that may have gotten lost in the abuse. If any part of your identity has been tainted by gaslighting, it's time to put it behind you.

Recovery

If you're the victim of gaslighting abuse, don't give up. It's so important to remember that there is no such thing as a perfect relationship; if you have one, then it's not yours. Your partner should support and help you grow into your best self and not manipulate you into believing what they think is real.

If your relationship feels like it's impossible to break out of, then reach out for help. You do not have to face it alone; there are many resources that can help you along your journey to freedom. You are worth the fight, and no one has the right to deny your reality but you.

Gaslighting can happen to anyone regardless of gender, age or position. However, it is a well-known fact that women are more prone to this type of abuse than men, and the three most common types of gaslighters are parents, siblings and partners. Older women (50–85 years) experience the highest rates of physical and sexual violence from younger male partners in intimate relationships when they are also experiencing ageism.

Gaslighting may be described as an extreme case of emotional abuse by manipulation. The abuser wants the victim to question their own feelings, instincts, and sanity by distorting the truth. Gaslighting abuse is often subtle. Its victims are led to question their own reactions through "family" or "friend" manipulation, usually portrayed as a joke, which can lead to anxiety, depression, and ultimately substance abuse problems. These can be the more severe manifestations of the abuse.

The victims of gaslighting don't recognize it as an act of violence until they have been deceived for so long that their former reality is distorted, and they think the new reality truly exists. This is often the reason why a victim doesn't come forward because they feel certain that no one would believe them.

The abuser also manages to make the victim's situation seem more critical than it actually is, which causes emotional distress. It is no wonder that the victim is more prone to using substances to cope with their situation or escape. Many abusers have even been known to exploit their victim's substance abuse problems for financial gain.

Chapter 4
Narcissist Target: Traits that Makes You a Prime Target for Narcissists

First, it is important to note that the popular notion that narcissists target weak, desperate women or men is nothing short of misleading. Also, being a victim of narcissistic abuse is never the victim's fault by any means. Narcissists are emotional predators and the fact that you're a human makes you automatically vulnerable to their antics. That said, it makes sense to identify the traits that narcissists identify in their targets so that potential victims can better protect themselves and sever ties early on, especially when they realize they are being targeted for exploitation.

When you consider these traits, you'll realize how wonderful they are, especially if allowed to blossom in a healthy and loving relationship. Sadly, a narcissist will only use them to manipulate, exploit ,and damage their victims. Below are some of the traits that narcissists look out for in potential victims:

1. Conscientiousness

2. Empathy

3. Integrity

4. Resilience

5. A high degree of sentimentality

6. Conscientiousness

Many people do not realize this, but one of the prime qualities a narcissist looks for is the ability of the potential victim to be conscientious. Truth be told, conscientious people are always concerned about the wellbeing of others, and they always carry out their obligation. The reason they are vulnerable to narcissists is that their decisions are tied to their conscience and, sadly, they project their sense of morality onto the narcissist, assuming that he will do the same.

Narcissists are very manipulative; they know how easy it is to exploit people who are conscientious enough to worry about other people's needs. They know that a conscientious person is one of the very few people that would grant them numerous chances, give them benefit of doubt, and even care more about them than their personal needs.

Narcissists love to target conscientious people for romantic relationships because they are aware of the fact that conscientious people see caretaking as an obligation, especially in relationships. They know that these people are ready to fulfill their obligations even if they feel endangered or if it puts them in harm's way.
Dr. George Simon, in his book, Personalities Prone to Narcissistic Manipulation, said that disturbed individuals most often target

those who possess two qualities that they, themselves, don't possess. These traits are excessive agreeableness being very conscientious. People with these traits tend to defer to others, such as the narcissist, by complying with their demands and manipulation. Ironically, those who possess a conscience are more vulnerable to those who do not. Shame and guilt are the primary tools or weapons used by those who manipulate others, but in order for that to work, you have to have the capacity for these traits in the first place.

Empathy

The joy of every narcissist is to encounter an empathic victim because narcissists, in general, do not get a constant narcissistic supply of attention, praise, resources, etc. from people who lack empathy - like themselves. Thus, the importance of securing a narcissistic target cannot be overemphasized.

Narcissists cannot show empathy towards others, but they carefully target people who have a great deal. The physical and emotional validation that empathic people give narcissists help maintain their bloated egos and feelings of authority, or else they practically starve and renew their hunt for a new source of supply.

When you put everything into consideration, you'll realize that empathic people are the opposite of narcissists, and their attitude helps to empower narcissists in their abuse cycle. For example, the fact that an empath is always willing to see the narcissist's perspective even at the height of abuse is something that maintains the abuse cycle over and over. As if that is not enough, narcissists identify with empathic people because they know that they're the ideal audience for their pity ploys even after highly abusive incidents.

If you happen to be an empathic person, understand that narcissists believe they can just put out a faux apology or sob story to write off their abuse. They know you'll always see reasons for their toxic behaviors and even make excuses on their behalf. They depend on your God-given ability to forgive and sympathize with them irrespective of the ill treatments they've subjected you to in the past.

Most times, narcissists escape retribution and accountability for their actions because they appeal to the empathy of their victims. It is very hard to pretend to be who you are not, and as such, empathic people, being who they are, always second-guess their decisions to punish the narcissists for their actions because they feel an unbearable amount of guilt when they see the narcissist prosecuted (either by society or law). Thus, they are always inclined to protect their abusers as opposed to exposing them to the world as to who they truly are.

Integrity

This might sound very funny, but narcissists are incredibly attracted to people who keep to their word. When they come in contact with people of integrity, they see a lot of attributes they can exploit for their own gain. For example, if it is not in the moral code of a victim to cheat or give up on a relationship prematurely, who stands to benefit? The narcissist, who is morally and mentally impoverished!

While the victims feel morally apprehensive about betraying the relationship, executing retaliation, or even withdrawing from their supposed obligations to the narcissists, the narcissist in question maintains zero remorse for harming their victims. The victim possesses a rare gift that can be of benefit to them and their partners in a healthy and productive relationship. However, this same gift becomes a weapon in the hands of a narcissist – a deadly weapon used to destroy their self-worth and self-belief.

Resilience

The most painful part about being a victim of narcissistic abuse is the realization that you weren't even wrong most times. As a victim of narcissistic abuse, your ability to bounce back from your abuser's acts is something that strengthens your bond with him. Resilient people, e.g. childhood abuse survivors, are highly effective sources for the narcissist because they have a very high threshold for pain and abuse.

Resilience is a very good quality to possess, especially when faced with adversities of life, but in an abusive relationship, the victim's resilience is exploited and used against him/her to keep them enslaved in the abuser's web of deceit and manipulation.

Even though resilient people are more aware of the dangers of their environments, they still find it difficult to give up on their abusers even after multiple incidents. Typically, they will choose to disregard their instincts and fight for their relationship by assuming the role of a "fighter" or "savior," as they put in energy to keep an unsustainable relationship afloat.

The saddest part about the resilient victim is that there are times when they even quantify their love by the amount of abuse they've suffered at the hands of their abusers. Unknown to them, this occurs because they have successfully developed an abuse bond with the toxic and abusive partner.

High degree of sentimentality

There is no gainsaying that narcissists are overbearing, petty, and manipulative. Thus, targets who are sentimental and capable of falling deeply in love, are extremely appealing to narcissists because they know they can use love-bombing (the use of extreme praise and flattery to groom a victim) to easily manipulate them.

During the early stages of narcissistic relationships, narcissists shower their victims with so much love and attention: the idea is to secure their trust and appeal to their craving for love. It is a strategy that works very well for them! They intentionally create sweet memories that they want their victims to romanticize during future periods of abuse.

Narcissists love to play with their victim's emotions; they know they can get their victims hooked before they start to withdraw by creating a fraudulent "soulmate" effect that will cripple their victims and leave them wanting things to be as they were during the early stages of the relationship.

Narcissists find it very easy to trick empathic and sentimental people – the only thing they do is fraud their victims into believing they're kicking off a meaningful, long-term relationship. It is very normal for people to want to maintain long term, healthy relationships, but it becomes a problem when a predatory narcissist is involved.

Why did the narcissist target you? You have something the narcissist wants (lifestyle, power, money, position). In a narcissistic relationship, certain things come into play. First of all, it begins with a hook – a dream – and most times you think it is all about you and your wellbeing, but the truth is that the narcissist is all about control.

There are occasions when the narcissist will appear to be helpful, but when things don't go as planned, the tables turn on you. However, when you realize the pattern and opt to hold the narcissist accountable for his actions, things get out of hands and degenerate rapidly.

Chapter 5
Coping with a Narcissist

Being able to identify a narcissist is just the beginning. Once you recognize that you have one in your life, the next step is knowing how to overcome the experience and its associated consequences. It can be emotionally and mentally challenging to be around a person with narcissism. It is imperative not to delay dealing with the situation properly to minimize potential negative effects.

Dealing with a Narcissist

Dealing with a narcissist is something that truly takes practice. It takes a different tack than those without narcissism, and since this is not an issue you deal with frequently with multiple people, there is a learning curve. Never discount yourself. This is what they want, but there are ways to ensure that you are creating and maintaining the right boundaries.

Do Not Give in to Their Fantasy

A narcissist builds a fantasy life, and when dealing with them, it is important not to fall into the fantasy. They can be charming so it can be hard to resist them. It does not take long to essentially get lost in their web. At first, you might feel important and special, but this never lasts. Keep the following in mind:

- They will not fulfill your needs. In fact, what you need and want will not even be recognized. A narcissist views your value as what you can do to satiate their ego.

- Pay attention to how they treat others. You will see that they are not afraid to manipulate, lie, disrespect and hurt other people. Eventually, this behavior and treatment will trickle down to you.

- While it is not easy, the rose-colored glasses have to come off to evaluate how they are truly treating you. When you care about someone, denial is the easiest route to take concerning their true character, but this has to be put aside.

- Don't forget about your dreams. When you are close to a narcissist, it is easy to get swept up in their delusions and fantasy. Do not lose yourself or you may find it hard to regain control.

Set Boundaries and Stick to Them

One of the biggest elements of a healthy relationship is setting healthy boundaries and sticking to them. Of course, a narcissist does not understand boundaries, so this can be tricky. Remember that your relationships with others should be built on a foundation of mutual respect and care. While you will not get what you give, you still have to approach the relationship like any other. This will reduce the chances of your boundaries being violated.

For example, a narcissist is not shy about taking what they want. You might have a female friend who is a narcissist who just raids your closet and takes anything at any time. In a normal friendship, this friend would ask first, but narcissists do not ask permission. They feel they deserve anything they want, and this includes anything you have.

If you have had a relationship with a narcissist for a while, you surely can see their pattern of not respecting boundaries. To change this, make a plan based on what you hope to achieve. Then, consider how you will enforce the plan and what the consequences will be should the narcissist violate your boundaries. The most important thing is that you stand firm and do not give into the needs of the narcissist. Let them know when your boundaries have been crossed.

Be prepared for relationship changes. A narcissist is not a big fan of people who don't admire them and give into their every whim. They want to call all the shots, and they want you to prop them up. Once you start creating boundaries, how they treat you is likely to change because they will not be happy about you standing up for yourself.

They may try to punish you, demean you, or go in the opposite direction and use fake charm to manipulate you into going back to giving them what they want. To maintain the friendship, you might take a gentle approach to boundary setting. For example, instead of just abruptly changing things and being harsh when explaining why, plan what to say and then deliver the message in a way that is clear, calm, gentle and respectful. If the conversation is not going as planned, simply walk away. Do not continue to engage or allow the person to try and manipulate you into going back to your old habits of giving in.

Avoid Taking Things Personally

This will be one of the hardest things you do, but it is important. A narcissist is not purposely trying to hurt you. This is just who they are, and they are unable to see fault in their behavior. Remember that their actions, behaviors, and emotions are not about you. It is all about them.

A narcissist will try and create a version of you that is easiest for them to control. Work on your self-esteem and know your worth so their view of you does not become how you see yourself. Let them keep their own negativity and do not allow it to change how you feel about yourself.

This also means that you need to know who you are. A narcissist is not able to admit that they have weaknesses, and they overinflate their strengths. However, you need to take an honest look at yourself. If a narcissist is attacking one of your strengths, you can simply walk away. You know it is something you are good at. Be proud of it and do not allow them to make you feel inferior.

Do not argue with them. This will be hard when the natural instinct is to defend yourself when someone is attacking you. Remember that a narcissist is not rational and no amount of logic will change this. Simply state calmly that you disagree and then walk away.

Lastly, never look to a narcissist for approval. Even if they tell you nice things, they are only doing it to manipulate and gain control over you. As long as you know your worth and have good self-esteem, you do not need them to approve of anything you do or think.

Find a Good Support System
A narcissist is never going to be a good support person for you. However, you do need support when dealing with someone like this in your life. If they are close to you and have been in your life

a while, the first step is learning what a healthy relationship is. It is about mutual respect and give and take. With a narcissist, you only give, and they only take.

Focus your time on those who give you love, respect, and honesty. This will help you to see who you truly are so you do not have to get approval from the narcissist in your life. Start to break away. A narcissist wants all attention, so they often isolate those they want to keep for themselves. This makes it easier for them to gain control over you. Spend time meeting new people or reconnecting with friends you might have lost touch with.

Seek out meaningful opportunities and activities. Consider going for that promotion you have wanted, volunteer, or try a new hobby. When you have a fulfilling life, its acts as a natural support system.

How to Treat a Narcissist

You want to start by distinguishing between a grandiose narcissist and a vulnerable one. When you are dealing with one that is vulnerable, they have a weak inner core they are masking with outward self-absorption and self-centeredness. The grandiose ones are not shy about how great they believe they are, and they truly believe they are the best.

Treating a narcissist in the right way is the easiest method to ensure that their negative behavior does not fall back on you and cause negativity in your life. To ensure that you are treating them in the right way, there are a number of things to do so you can evaluate them and develop the best strategy.

Determine the Narcissist's Type

You want to know if you are dealing with a vulnerable or grandiose narcissist. This makes it possible to determine what is needed to get the best response from them. For example, the grandiose type feels they are the best, so they need their ego stroked. On the other hand, the vulnerable type needs to feel special at all times due to their fragile ego. They need constant praise and reassurance.

Acknowledge How Annoyed You Are

Narcissists can really get into your skin, causing you to be annoyed with them. They want all of the attention, so they commonly interrupt you when you are doing anything other than giving them attention. Do not just blow this off. Instead, acknowledge that their behavior annoys you so you can start putting a stop to it.

Consider the Context

In many cases, certain situations trigger the worst narcissistic behavior. For example, you have a coworker who desperately wanted a promotion, but someone else got it. If she is a narcissist, this rejection may cause her to become very insecure, and in some cases, angry. This would result in her becoming spiteful, vindictive and downright difficult to deal with.

Know the Source of the Behavior

A narcissist does not think like everyone else. For those without narcissism, getting over insecurities is not overly difficult. It is just part of healthy coping. However, with a narcissist, they essentially need to have their ego rebuilt after a situation that caused them to feel inferior. It is important to balance how you treat them after a tough time.

For example, you are working on a school project with someone who is a narcissist. Something happens that exposes a weakness. This breaks their ego and can make them just stop working on the project, but you still need their contribution. To get them back on track, give them balanced reassurance. Too much and their ego can quickly get too big again, so approach the situation with this in mind.

Do Not Allow the Narcissist to Derail You

When you are doing something that takes attention away from them, they might try to sabotage you so that you stop doing it and get back to making them number one. It is important that you keep your goal upfront and do not allow anything they do or say to stop you from pursuing your goal or doing what you want to do.

For example, you and the narcissist usually do something together on Friday nights. However, you decide you want to start taking a class on your own. Since this takes your attention away from them, they may try to do things to get you to quit taking your class. Do not give in.

Make Sure to Stay Positive

Narcissists feed on watching other people feel bad, so even if they cause you to experience negative emotions, do not let them see this. When you are around them, make sure you are in a positive mindset. No matter how hard they try to bring you down, keep a smile on your face and do not react.

Call Their Bluff

Remember that the narcissist wants to keep you down because this makes it easier for them to control you. When they are trying to do something negative, do not give in and do not get offended. Instead, walk away or laugh. They want to see you upset, so if you do not do this in front of them, it starts to take away some of their control.

Know That They Need Help

Narcissism is a mental health issue that someone cannot just be willed away. They will need help if they ever expect to get their behavior under control. If you approach them and recommend they reach out to a professional, they are unlikely to agree and go. They may even become angry or defensive. If you care about the person and want them to at least consider help, approach the subject gently and know that this is something you will likely have to discuss several times before they will even consider it.

Freeing Yourself from Negative Emotions

Anger, jealousy, envy and other negative emotions can permeate your life and cause significant problems. It is important to recognize their existence and then work to be free of them. Freeing yourself from such emotions is a process, and it takes time. Even after you free yourself, you will need to commit to long-term work and maintenance.

Negative emotions are powerful and can quickly become habits if you do not get them under control. For example, if you commonly respond to criticism with anger, over time, this repetition will cause you to become angry any time you are criticized. This can start to impact your relationships, your career, and other elements of your life.

Stop Justifying

Stop justifying your negative emotions. If you are getting angry all of the time, take responsibility for why and stop trying to place the blame elsewhere. Anger is a very powerful emotion that can quickly become a habit. As soon as you recognize that this habit is problematic and admit it is not good, you can start to reevaluate why you are feeling this way so you can change it.

Stop Making Excuses

When you make excuses for negative emotions, either for yourself or others, you are telling yourself that they are out of your control. This is not true because you have the choice as to how you react to a situation. If you continue to make excuses, you will never take responsibility for your behavior. Over time, this can start to push people out of your life because they will not want to be around someone who cannot admit their faults or when they are wrong.

Take Responsibility

Once you dedicate yourself to no longer making excuses, you can start to take some responsibility for how you act in various situations. This starts by taking the power away from your negative emotions. As you continue to take responsibility, you will find that they lose their hold over you. The right reactions and choices will naturally start to become easier to make.

Do Not Overanalyze Other People's Opinions of You

Your emotions are your responsibility, but external factors can make them a bit harder to control. One of the biggest external factors is how other people view you. This is especially true if someone is especially vocal in criticizing you. This is often what narcissists do to keep you under their control.

Humans naturally want to be wanted and loved. When someone you respect or care about says something negative about you, the natural reaction is to go on the offensive. However, you want to instead hear what they are saying and then determine if it is true.

For example, did your supervisor yell at you for making a small error on a work project? Consider why they yelled. Think about the big picture. Okay, you made a small mistake, but overall, you completed the project and did well with it. Remember this and allow the yelling to roll off your back.

Stop Your Bad Habits

Any bad habit you have can add to the negatively in your life. For example, eating fast food often, smoking or not maintaining good dental hygiene. Take time to write down your bad habits. Once you put them in writing, they are easier to recognize. Start by working on one at a time because it is easier to correct a bad habit when you put a lot of focus on it. When you work to enhance your total wellbeing, your emotions will benefit.

Cut Off Negative People

If people in your life are largely a negative influence, walk away. It does not matter how close you are or how long you have known the person. When they are constantly negative, this is not doing any good for your life. If you really care about the person, you can consider talking to them. However, not everyone can change, and some may just not want to. For example, a narcissist is not able to just stop their negative behavior. It is a part of their personality. Because of this, simply talking to them is not likely to get you anywhere.

Think Before Responding

Negative emotions are powerful, so it is not uncommon for them to spill out. However, train yourself to wait 10 seconds before responding to a situation that causes negative emotions. This allows you to calm down so your response is appropriate for the situation. For example, you were supposed to meet a friend for dinner, and you were an hour late. They are upset. Instead of just responding back in anger and getting into a fight, count to 10 and then consider why they are mad. It will be easier to see that they did nothing wrong and you should apologize.

Be Grateful

Even during the worst of times, you have awesome things in your life that you should be grateful for. When you put your focus on them, it helps to alleviate the negative feelings. Consider keeping a journal and at the end of each day, take a few minutes to write down all the good things that happened that day. Over time, the positive elements of your life will start to naturally outweigh the negative.

Stop Saying, "I Can't"

If you keep telling yourself that you cannot do something, you will eventually start to believe it. This is what is referred to as a self-fulfilling prophecy. Give yourself credit and stop limiting yourself to what is easy and in your comfort zone. As you push yourself and see how many things you are truly good at, it will put you in a more positive frame of mind, naturally pushing out the negative emotions.

Let It Go

Life would be much simpler if everything could be controlled, but this is not possible. When you find something you have no control over, recognize it and let it go. For example, not every person will like you, and there are times when a loved one may get mad at you for something that is not your fault. Do not press the issue. Let go, and everything will eventually work itself out.

There are simple things you can start doing on a regular basis to push out negative emotions and enhance your overall wellbeing. You do not have to do every single one on a daily basis but consider them and incorporate some into your day when appropriate.

- Be proactive and do not allow the negative to settle into your life

- When life gets tough, cry it out because this aids in reducing stress

- Scream as loud as you can for a few seconds as this naturally counteracts negative emotions

- Get some sleep since it is easier to tackle stress and negative emotions when you are not exhausted

- Try to be positive and no matter what happens, force yourself to find the silver lining in the situation

- Take a few minutes to laugh every day since when you are laughing, negative emotions cannot be present

- Find someone you trust who cares about you and talk to them when you need to get help with a problem

- Consider an alternate perspective to see if it might allow you to better solve a problem

- Forgive yourself for setbacks as long as you recognize them and do not allow them to completely throw you off track

- Own your feelings and when negative emotions occur, recognize them, consider why you are experiencing them, and then detach from it

- Write about the day or experience you just had before going to bed each night as this allows you to leave the negative in the past so you can start fresh the next day

Chapter 6
Surviving Narcissistic Abuse

No matter how a relationship of this nature has put you down or worn you out, you can rise again. Despite the abuse and strife and all the mind games, you can come out strong and regain your sanity. Narcissism exists in different phases of life relationships. It is not only peculiar to romantic relationships; narcissism exists in business and at work, among families, siblings, and friends. But before we explore this, we should talk about the psychological effects of narcissism on its victims.

Impact of Narcissism on the Brain

Many people find themselves stuck in abusive relationships. It could be emotionally abusive parents, a friendship or romantic relationship. The effect is almost the same, which is more than mere emotional and physiological damage. Neuroscientists have revealed that narcissistic abuse can cause physical brain damage in victims.

When exposed to emotional trauma for an extended period, it can trigger symptoms of PTSD. This is why the remedy for abusive relationships is to leave. Walk away before you lose your entire self to this person. Unknown to many, the long-term effect of narcissism is way more than emotional and psychological distress.

What many do not know is that the brain is actually damaged by regular exposure to emotional abuse. With this prolonged exposure to abuse, the amygdala can swell and some experience a reduction in the size of the hippocampus (Morey, 2012.) The after-effect of this is horrible, but to understand why, we must understand the role of the amygdala and hippocampus.

The amygdala is responsible for negative emotions such as fear, anxiety, worry, guilt, and shame. The hippocampus helps in the formation of memories as well as learning. To effectively learn as humans, we should be able to retain information into our short-term memory. This is the first step in learning. This needs to happen before any information gets transferred to long-term memory. In other words, short-term memory is as crucial to learning as long-term memory.

Damage to the hippocampus produces a devastating effect. According to a study at the University of New Orleans and Stanford University, a reduction of the hippocampus is linked to high levels of cortisol (a stress hormone) in the body (Carrion, 2007.) In other words, excess stress in people makes the hippocampus smaller.

The amygdala, known as the reptilian brain, is in charge of emotions such as fear, hate, lust, etc. It is also related to breathing and heart rate. It is responsible for triggering the fight and flight response. Victims of narcissistic abuse are always in a state where their amygdala is on high alert. With time, these people transition to a state where fear and anxiety become a constant, and the amygdala will pick up on the slightest sign of abuse.

Even after the victim has left the abusive relationship, there are lingering signs of post-traumatic stress such as panic attacks and excessive phobias. This is because the amygdala's increased size now considers the state of fear and anxiety as normal. To try and keep themselves from the reality of the situation, victims use reality twisting devices such as:

Projection: in a bid to try and deny the facts, victims choose to believe that the narcissist is not all bad. They want to believe deep down that there is some compassion. Most of the time, this is a lie.
Denial: victims refuse to accept the gravity of their situation. They convince themselves that living with it is better than any confrontation.
Compartmentalization: victims ignore the abusive aspects of the relationship and choose to focus only on the positive ones.

The Gradual Damage of the Hippocampus

The hippocampus helps us read, study, understand, and process information. In other words, the hippocampus handles everything related to learning and knowledge. Since it relates to learning, it is associated with the formation of new memories.

This crucial part of the brain is negatively affected by stress due to the presence of cortisol. Cortisol decreases the size of the hippocampus, making us more subjected to stress and anxiety. The more these distressing emotions thrive in the brain, the more our brain is changed.

Stress from narcissistic abuse, both of a short and long-term stress duration, are equally damaging. As a result, even subtle abuse and manipulation from the abuser can destroy the victim's brain. With many methods of healing available to those who experience abuse, you can reconfigure the brain to have a normal reaction to stress.

Surviving Narcissistic Abuse in Families

Do either of these scenarios sound familiar?

- A mother tells her daughter that no man will want her if she is fat
- A father lies to his children and dismisses their opinions, all to get them to do things for him

Some level of narcissism is prevalent in most families. There are many tactics a narcissist's parents could choose to exert control over their children. This often has a profound effect on the child, creating deep and painful wounds on the child's mental state. Being raised by a narcissistic parent can be devastating and potentially degenerating, causing low self-esteem if left unaddressed by the adult.

Naturally, it is believed that love should be instilled in all parents. There should be this unbroken bond that connects parents to their children. Looking specifically at the kind of intimacy a child shares with the mother, you expect to find an unbreakable chord of love that brings them together. However, not every mother is capable of unconditional love.

Some parents have been so eaten away by their past traumas that they don't see their children as special human beings deserving of their love. Instead, these parents only see them as extensions of themselves. This explains why they perceive their children as competition, a source of jealousy, and sometimes even a threat.

To narcissistic parents, their youngsters are objects that hinder their personal needs. Being raised by a narcissistic parent can be devastating for a child. However, healing is possible as soon as the child realizes it's important. You don't need to spend a lifetime trying to mend your broken and damaged self-esteem due to your parents. To heal, you have to:

<u>Mourn</u>: you were robbed of the normal childhood every kid deserves. Remember this and mourn properly as you would when losing something important.

<u>Accept:</u> you see another child's mother and wish yours was like her. You need to accept that your life is just different from others, and that's okay. Your upbringing has little to do with you; it was just an unfortunate turn to be born into a broken home, devoid of love and normal human emotions. You need to accept that this is who your parents were and make the best of it.

The process of grieving and accepting is primal to healing. This is not about healing the relationship with your parents but the relationship with yourself. Continuous exposure to abuse or neglect from your parents may have eroded your self-esteem, lowered your confidence, or made you feel unworthy of love, but there's always a chance to improve. The love, care, and attention you never received from your parents can instead come from you.

Other healing techniques are:

Get Rid of Your Inner Critic

During the abuse while with your parents, you believed they might love and accept you if you were more talented or smarter. When this never happened, you resolved that you were clearly unlovable. This left the voices of your parents in your head always criticizing and being negative. Allowing behavior like this to continue will only start a cycle of shame and abuse. Be kind to yourself and understand that no one is perfect.

Embrace Your Inner Child

You may think blocking it out is the way to cope. Nope. Think deeply about your feelings at this time. Look inward and see yourself when you were criticized and felt unloved. Embrace this helpless child and develop a strong, safe, loving relationship with that person - it is you after all. Rather than constantly criticizing yourself, try to see your flaws in a different way. With warmth and acceptance, embrace this poor damaged kid with compassion.

Exercise Self-Care

Living and growing up with narcissistic parents might have conditioned you not to focus on your needs. You only seek to please and do what you think makes them happy. As a result, you are completely lost on how to embrace your needs.

Fix this by treating yourself. Do something just for you and spend time alone to really begin to love for yourself, maybe an activity or adventure that makes you nothing but happy. You and your needs matter. Considering that a child spends an average of fifteen years living under the pressure of a parent, with narcissists, that time might feel like an eternity. Abuse doesn't happen overnight or over the span of a year, so the journey to recovery can be long and at times hard. Good things take time, so allow yourself to take the time you need while being surrounded by people you love. In time, you will see visible improvements in every aspect of your life; developing a healthy and loving relationship with yourself and others are just the baby steps you need to begin.

Healing Narcissistic Abuse in Relationships

Suffering mental, physical, and emotional abuse at the hands of a narcissist can be one of the most challenging things to get through. It affects every part of the victim's life, eroding their confidence and making them doubt themselves. Constant attacks with no relief or time for the mind and body to process the attack, let alone heal, is why many people end up with symptoms of PTSD.

The following steps can help the healing begin:

Create Ironclad Boundaries

To heal yourself from an abusive relationship, you need an imaginary barricade to keep the negativity out, in the form of boundaries. This is the foundation for your healing journey to get off the ground. Thinking you're out of the fray leaves you vulnerable to the narcissist, potentially giving them another chance to mess with your head. This contact can trigger pain that can pose as a major setback.

While the best method is to physically stay away from them, you can also give them the cold shoulder or just ignore them if getting away isn't easy. Leave no opportunity for them to prey on your emotions. Be emotionally distant even while interacting with them. You also need to learn object. This is a gradual way to build your self-esteem and regain your confidence.

Forgive Yourself

Some part of you knew all along that something was not right, but you were so drunk in love you didn't realize. This can make you shoulder the blame and be too hard on yourself. This won't help. Anybody could have been the victim, you were just in the right position to get in bed with a broken person. You were manipulated, tricked, and brainwashed. You could not have seen it coming even if there were a ton of warning signs. Realize that you are a whole person, full of love and deserving of love. You are kind, smart, and worthy. It is the narcissist's loss for not knowing your true worth.

Adjust Your Focus

Having spent a lot of time with your abuser, there will an overload of moments to reflect on. This is a trauma bond—a sign that there are unprocessed emotions you need to deal with. The idea here is to find time to work on them with mindful intention, rather than being dragged by your past forever. Embrace mindfulness and engage in visualizations of a bright and hopeful future.

The narcissist may have made you bench your dreams for theirs, but it's time for you to start working on them again. With a revitalized sense of purpose, you can get rid of the lingering thoughts of abuse that will hold you back.

Release the Abuser

The relationship with an abuser is often filled with anxiety and fear. You walk on eggshells anxious that the next thing you want to do will trigger their rage, causing a fight and a further unpleasant situation. There is a tendency for this to continue long after separation from the narcissist.

While we do not doubt the fact that narcissists love losing and can be stubborn in their pursuit, realize that they are not as strong as you think. They only want you to believe they are. With this in mind, the ability to get rid of the trauma bond will help you disarm them. You can now become established and resolute, unwavering even in the face of all their issues and drama.

Practice Mindfulness

When you stay sin an abusive relationship, you subconsciously transport yourself into a state of hyper-vigilance. You are always careful of your moves, afraid of doing anything to spook your abuser. This creates excessive stimulation of the sympathetic system, which leads to an influx of adrenaline and other stress chemicals into the blood.

The key to deactivate this is to activate the parasympathetic system. In other words, you are transitioning from fight or flight mode to rest mode. This comes from various methods such as deep breathing, mindfulness, or any activity that relaxes and eases your anxiety.

All in all, know that you can heal and break free from the shackles of an abusive relationship. Your effort to heal and recover yourself can be the ticket to a whole, integrated, and complete human being. You can improve!

Narcissism Among Friends

Friendship is a beautiful gift. You choose those that surround you, and these friends help make the world seem a little brighter and life worth living. Friends are there to catch us when we fall, and the people we are close to receive the investment of our trust and emotions. This bond can be overlooked by many, taking it for granted.

However, there are some instances where disturbing patterns, pain, and an unhealthy attachment seem to characterize the friendship. Some people are trapped in a narcissistic friendship without any idea of what that means, just that they are unhappy. Believing in someone's goodness is a basic premise of humanity. You hang on for the ride, longing for the friend you once knew to come back. Unfortunately, there are times when things can never go back.

Holding on too long can open you up to narcissistic abuse. Due to the attachment, our narcissist friend finds it easy to prey and impose on us. They see us as an extension of themselves, and nothing we ever do is good or acceptable. Worst of all, you never seem to agree on anything as your narcissist friend believes their opinions are more important, and right.

Rather than enjoying the benefit that comes from having a friend, the benefits of the relationship are one-sided. You are there to meet their needs and soothe their ego. Saying sorry is not in their dictionary, and they will never accept that they have done anything wrong. Holding on to this friendship for long starts taking its toll. By desperately trying to fix a broken friendship, we drown. Our self-worth, self-esteem and self-confidence will suffer for it. The relationship becomes draining and you are exhausted, trying to salvage it.

Narcissism is real and plagues every facet of human relationships. Even though it is a lot to take in, many people find themselves in this kind of relationship. It is disappointing and shocking that such a thing could occur among friends, but that is the reality. If you have found yourself in this kind of relationship, here are some tips to keep your sanity intact:

<u>Be Good to Yourself</u>: you do not need another person to complete you. Any friend that takes advantage of you should be cut out of your life. Realize that friendship does not add value to you and is not worth the time.

<u>Free Yourself</u>: while there is nothing wrong with trying to help your friend, know when to draw the line. This might be difficult because letting go of a friend isn't always easy. But what friendship is worth the exhaustion?

<u>Know What You Will Tolerate</u>: narcissists, even in friendship, sees everyone as less than themselves. In their world, they are superior, so they expect to be treated like it. They also operate with the mindset that they can treat everyone like trash and a nobody.

Know your self-worth and what you will not tolerate from your friend. Know when to draw the line.

<u>Know When to Get Help</u>: being in a narcissistic relationship is complicated and draining. It takes its toll on almost all areas of life. There are times you might need to seek outside help in order to recover from the anguish of dealing with a narcissist. There are support groups, and therapy can be of help.

<u>Knowing when to walk away</u> from a friend or relationship takes courage. It can be a lot to process, which hurts. However, you need to protect yourself from a friendship that drains the life out of you.

Workplace Narcissism

Narcissists are peculiar people, and they are easy to spot from an outsider's perspective. They occur in every facet of human interactions, including the workplace. They are typically obnoxious, overly outspoken and can make everyone around them uncomfortable. Using various manipulation techniques like mind control, they find it easy to get people entangled in their webs. As master manipulators, they can put up a front to get on the good side of people. They are charismatic, the life of the party, risk-takers, and they know how to get others to do things for them. This makes it easy for them to rise to a leadership position.

With narcissists, all that glitters is not gold. You need to know how to protect yourself from all their mind games and manipulations. We have the following tips to protect yourself from the narcissist

How to Spot a Narcissist

This is perhaps the most important part of surviving narcissism in the workplace. You need to keep yourself updated on the signs of a narcissist so you will not be caught in their traps. Narcissists are skilled at blending in to get what they want, and developing an ability to see past their veil will help. They might come off as friendly and charismatic at first. But as we have learned, they love making friends with people they can easily take advantage of.

They believe everything they do is under the radar so calling a narcissist out on their behavior might end up backfiring. They like to employ tactics like guilt, gaslighting, and criticism to create any type of chaos in their power, even in professional settings such as the workplace. Watch out for this.

Get Your Facts Right

If the narcissist your boss, confrontation might not be the best tactic. They are not against using dark tactics to confuse and disorient you, creating an unpleasant work situation and eventually getting rid of any threats.

Letting things go is not in their nature. With this in mind, you need to be smarter in your dealings with thing. Keep tabs on everything, all you observe, what they do and say. This will go a long way in protecting you and making a case for your arguments when the time comes.

Guard Your Weaknesses

Empaths and narcissists make for a toxic relationship because narcissists see the caring and nurturing nature of the empaths as a weakness. They see these as a loophole to get attached and entangled with them. If the empath knows their forgiving nature could get them into trouble, it's a good plan to keep this fact hidden.

In other words, a narcissist will draw near you if they feel there is something they can take advantage of. This calls for knowing yourself and the attributes that make you vulnerable. If you trust people easily, have trouble saying no and do things for people freely, the narcissist might explore these traits and use them to their advantage.

Avoid Taking Things Personally

In the world of narcissists, they are the most important person. They do not care about who gets hurt and who they victimize with their games. This is just how they are wired, and it is not your fault. It boils down to their need to put others down to feel better.

With this in mind, do not feel sad or bitter if they make derogatory comments or try to belittle you. It's just their insecurity showing.

Throughout the book, we have made sure not to recommend confrontation with this type of personality as it can only end in more problems. You might not win if you call them out. Stroking their ego, while being a step ahead of them, is a good way to protect yourself. Keep these points in mind and know how to play your cards right.

Chapter 7
Helping a Narcissist Recover

You might wonder why we are talking about how you can help someone with narcissism when we have spent so long telling you that you can't fix them. That isn't the point. We're not suggesting that you can wave a magic wand and fix this person, allowing them to have meaningful and lasting relationships and friendships. We're suggesting that there are ways you can at least help someone, and maybe encourage them seek help.

Know right now that it might not work; narcissists are by their very nature very stubborn and are not going to accept help if they don't deem it to be strictly necessary. By suggesting that they may have a problem and need help, you are (in their eyes) attacking their very personality and self, and that will not be taken lightly.

Narcissists aren't always 100% narcissistic; you might have someone who only has narcissism when certain events trigger it, e.g. when they're rejected or go through a hard time, and as a result, their personality disorder comes to the fore. On the other hand, you might be dealing with someone who is narcissistic all the time, but not to a huge degree. These are the people you may be able to help, but for anyone who is 100% severe and toxic in terms of narcissism, don't even bother trying. These people will not take your suggestion well, and the only way that these types of narcissistic will ever receive help is when they take everything a step too far.

So, in what ways can you actually attempt to help a narcissist? There are very few ways, but you can try and encourage them to seek help by subtle moves. Again, this depends on the type of narcissism. You should also be very prepared for rejection, but know that at least you tried. From there, you can figure out your own options and decide what your own plan of action is going to be. Remember, you can't change someone else without their will; you can only control yourself.

There are three main ways you can attempt to help someone close to you who is clearly in the grips of NPD.

Do Not Allow Them to Manipulate You

This particular step is for you mainly, but it does help them indirectly. By refusing to let them manipulate you, and by allowing their gaslighting attempts to backfire, you're actually making them sit up and take notice. They will see that you are stronger, and they will wonder why. They will not want you to leave, as they need you around, even though their behavior probably shows otherwise.

In some ways, dealing with a narcissist is like dealing with a child.

If you tell them they can't have something, but then give in, they'll simply continue that level of behavior because they know you'll give in at some point. Narcissists will do the same thing, which is why it is so important that if you say you're going to walk out of the room when they belittle you, you actually do it. Do not apologize for something that isn't your fault and do not bow down to their demands. This will take practice, and it will be hard, but by looking after yourself and your own needs first, you will find the strength to do it.

By ensuring that their tactics backfire, you're taking away a huge amount of their power. This could go one of two ways : they could turn angry and simply lash out at your attempts, or they could possibly start to soften. It depends on the level of narcissism they are afflicted with. Of course, if they lash out, cut your losses and walk away. You've tried, and there's nothing more you can do.

Wait Until They are Calm, and Have a Discussion

If you've tried step one and it didn't go badly, e.g. they softened a little, then perhaps this second step will help. Remember that in order for someone to seek help, it has to be their decision. It's no good forcing someone to see a doctor if they don't believe anything is wrong with them. Think about an alcoholic, for instance. You can't force this person to admit they need help. The first step towards recovery is knowing there is a problem in the first place.

The types of treatment for NPD all hinge on a total commitment to the treatment at hand. If someone doesn't really believe they need help, the treatment isn't going to work at all. So, the point of this step is to simply sow a seed in their mind and help them explore the possibilities.

Wait until they are calm to sit down and have a conversation. Be soft and don't be forceful. Talk to them, not at them, and make sure that you keep your emotions on an even keel. Tell them that you feel like they're treating you in an unfair way and give examples to back up your words. Tell them that you know they don't mean to treat you this way and they are a good person. If they remain calm, you may be able to make progress. If they simply throw a narcissistic tantrum and turn it around, again, you can't do anymore.

Find some literature on NPD and leave it on the table. Tell them that you've found this information and perhaps they might like to read it. Suggest you read it together, or they can read it on their own, and you'll be by their side whatever they decide.

Remember, it's not 100% guaranteed that this step will work, but it's worth a try if you want to know you did all you could before you decide to walk away. It's also important that by some stroke of luck, they agree to perhaps talk about things over with a health professional, and they recognize there might be something not quite right. Then you remain supportive and on their side at all times. Remember that deep down, a narcissistic is lacking in confidence and needs constant reassurance. The fact that you've suggested there might be something wrong could go either way, but by being calm and supportive - being on their side at all times - you may be able to guide them through it and toward professional help.

Issue an Ultimatum

This is the final method to try, and it's not one you should attempt as the first port of call. This is not likely to go well, but there is a chance. By issuing an ultimatum, you're basically saying, "look, I do not want to be treated in this way, but I know it's now what you really mean to do deep down. I'm giving you one chance to sort this out, and I will be by your side all the way. If you refuse, and if you continue to act in this way, I will leave for good."

You have to go through with your ultimatum and do not attempt to go back on it. Be strong and see it through, whatever way it goes. The point of this, however, is not to shout and lecture, it's a firm statement of intent. If you add emotions and hysterics, they are not going to take you seriously.

These are the only ways you can attempt to help someone with NPD, without actually being a health professional. Even if you were a health professional, the person would need to be willing to seek help and make a commitment to really putting in the effort to change. Treatment for NPD is quite intensive and requires a lot of deep thinking and behavioral change. It requires a strong will to make it work, so you can see why someone being forced to seek help is not going to have a good outcome.

The Importance of Knowing You Cannot "Save" Anyone

We've said this once, and we need to say it again. You cannot "save" a person with NPD, and you cannot fix them. This intention can only come from themselves. It's sad to walk away from someone who has a condition and doesn't actually "mean" to act in a certain way, but at the same time, you can't wave a magic wand and make it all go away again either.

The only thing you can do is focus on yourself and go with what you feel is right. You know in your gut that you deserve happiness and if your partner/friend or whoever this person is to you is not going to give you that, the only thing you can do for yourself is walk away. If you are in a relationship with this person, what would happen if children come into the equation? Would you want them to be born into a relationship with a large narcissistic element? That is certainly something to think about.

Make sure you have this fact in your mind before you attempt to help someone with NPD and before you make a decision to walk away. By knowing that in a solid and firm manner, you won't have regrets about your final actions.

Highly narcissistic people are usually unaware that they are so as they live very often in a state of denial and are unlikely to attempt to improve or work on themselves.

The Future for a Narcissist Who Refuses Help

It doesn't paint a great picture if the person isn't willing to seek help. In that case, it's far more likely that the narcissist will end up jumping from destructive relationship to destructive relationship, and if they do end up in a long-term union, it's unlikely that their partner will be truly happy and fulfilled. That person is far more likely to be simply "putting up" with the narcissism.

If a narcissist ends up in a relationship that yields children, the sad truth is that their children are quite likely to develop narcissistic tendencies as a result during their early years. While there isn't a certain answer to what causes NPD, there a definite suggestion that childhood experiences create a firm link to the personality in their adolescent and then adult years.

Narcissists also have the habit of becoming quite bitter over time. This is partly because people have come into their lives and left them, and they can't see why. Of course, they will project the blame onto the other person and don't see their role in them leaving. Many narcissistic traits, therefore, worsen with age, as more experiences are racked up throughout life.

As you can see, it's quite a bleak picture we're painting. and that is the sad truth about life as a narcissist. People can only stand being treated a certain way for so long before they eventually pluck up the courage to leave. While some never get to that point, these relationships are likely to be empty and lacking in true love and respect. For these reasons, the biggest price a narcissist pays for their actions over time is loneliness and a lack of a truly meaningful relationships in the end. For a narcissistic, however, the most loving and deep relationship they have is with themselves.

Chapter 8
The Narcissist and Empathy

When it's Time to Leave

At this point, your partner must be willing to at least try to make some changes in their behavior to improve their own mental health and the relationship. If your partner is willing to do some of the work, then your relationship can be saved. But, if you have been engaging in the activities discussed previously in this book, and your partner still does not see any problem with their behavior, there isn't much hope for an improvement.

Unfortunately, as much as we want to believe that we can change another person, we cannot always do so. You can change the dynamics on your end, which can improve the relationship for you, but in order for your partner to truly overcome their narcissistic traits, they have to put in some effort on their own. This chapter will outline some of the things that your partner can do to improve their narcissistic tendencies. These techniques are the last step to turn a narcissist into a loving and attentive partner.

Identify the Maladaptive Behaviors that Need to be Changed

What types of behaviors does your partner see as maladaptive or problematic? This could come from a list that you make or your partner understands to be true, or a combination of both. Once your partner acknowledges the inappropriate behaviors, he or she can begin to attack and alter them head on.

Once you both know and understand the types of behaviors to work on, you can set up a positive and negative reinforcement system. Basically, if your partner does something positive to change their behavior, they should be rewarded somehow, and if they engage in one of the behaviors you are trying to get rid of, a form of negative reinforcement (often called punishment) should be used like the "No Contact" principle. It works when, for instance, your partner gets abusive, and you distance yourself from him or her to protect yourself and cool things off. Your partner will eventually realize his or her mistake and will ask you to deal with the problem.

The punishments and rewards should be worked out between you both, and your partner has to be willing to commit to them. Many studies have shown that positive reinforcement works better than negative long term, so it makes sense to reward all small behaviors. If these rewards involve both of you, it could be a great way to strengthen your bond.

Practice Service to Others

People can learn to care for others. They have to choose to put the needs of another person before their own needs. If your narcissistic partner is willing to try this, it will be the first step to a more loving partnership. To do so, your partner should put aside one of their needs and do something for you no matter how simple or small. Whether it means running an errand that you usually do, making dinner, or taking care of one small thing so you don't have to, ask your partner to do something just for you. Start with something small, and over time, your partner will develop the ability to do more and more.

If your partner is willing to do these things for you, it is a good sign that they are willing to change. Talking about each other's needs and deciding the boundaries on both sides of the relationship is important. If your partner is amenable to do things for you, you, yourself, should be ready to do things for them as well, especially with regard to their mental health and stability. As discussed earlier, you have the right to say no to unreasonable demands, but, in a loving relationship, you have to give as well. But it must be reasonable.

Your partner will learn that providing a service to others will benefit both of you, and your partner will experience personal joy from seeing you happy, but it takes practice. Service to others is important to develop empathy for another person, which is the next step in the process.

Practice Empathy

Simply defined, empathy is the ability to put yourself in another person's place. By imagining how another person feels, you can relate to them better. The narcissist needs to do this, and it is a skill that takes practice. You can facilitate this by explaining to your partner how you feel when they do a certain thing. As they begin to understand this, they will be better able to put themselves in the position of another. Once your partner can understand how another person feels, they will be more likely to help them.

Don't Take Life so Seriously

To someone with narcissism, not getting their way seems like a life and death situation. But examining what happens if the narcissist doesn't get their way makes it easier to understand that horrible things will most likely not happen. The narcissist needs to remind themselves that they are not perfect, and they do not have to be. They need to look for the humor in little things. As soon as they learn not to take life so seriously, humor can be found. And tomorrow, it probably won't even be that important.

Once your partner realizes that even though yesterday seemed like a life and death situation, it's not the same as the present situation, and it will become easier to laugh at their own mistakes and move forward in a more loving way. When everything is no longer about them and they face the fact that they cannot get everything they want and learn that it is not a crisis, things will get easier. They will learn to let go of things and move on more easily. Your partner will learn that they do not have to have control of everything and that life will not fall apart.

Practice Self-Compassion

If your narcissist is the grandiose type, it is all the more important to practice self-compassion rather than develop self-esteem. Your narcissistic partner already has plenty of confidence, and this is what makes them think they are entitled to everything they want and desire. Instead, fostering self-compassion will help promote tenderness for other people. And, in the end, what will cause your partner to change their behavior is understanding that everyone deserves love and respect. It starts with loving and respecting themselves.

To foster self-compassion, consider the three steps: developing self-kindness, understanding our common humanity, and practicing mindfulness.

Self-kindness is the simple idea that we should not beat ourselves up when something goes wrong. It means that when we talk to ourselves in our mind, it should be kind, rather than harsh. If you or your partner makes a mistake, what thoughts go through your mind? Do you berate yourself or do you try to comfort yourself? Most narcissists will berate themselves and then lash out to try and make they feel better. Instead of lashing out at themselves, they should practice saying kind things in their mind. Remind yourself that everyone makes mistakes and it's okay not to be perfect because no one is. Say nice things to yourself.

Second, realizing that everyone faces the same struggles will help to connect to that common bond we call humanity. Everyone has imperfections. Everyone feels insecure at times, and everyone has problems. When you practice self-compassion, you put yourself on the same level with everyone else around you. This is a necessary step for the narcissist. When they are able to do this, they can stop treating everyone else as if they are only meant to serve their needs. They will realize that they are part of a greater whole, not above it. This will make it easier for them to change their behaviors. This is a key realization to turn a narcissist into a loving human being: that everyone comes from the same place and has issues from various roots. No one's problems or ideas are more important than another's.

Lastly, the narcissist must learn to practice mindfulness which means keeping their thoughts in the present moment. It also means acknowledging their feelings as they happen and thus dealing immediately with them. Suppressing what one thinks and feels causes emotional outbursts later. By dealing with them in the present moment, the narcissist will be less likely to act out in negative ways.

By working through these steps, the narcissist can be turned into a thoughtful and loving person. Self-compassion, when practiced regularly, will naturally transform into compassion for the world around them. It will need much effort and will take time. Doing these things is not an easy, but the benefits for both the narcissist, and you, as the partner, will be immensely gratifying.

Understanding Gas Lighting

Gas lighting comes from the movie of the same name that was released in 1944. It refers to a manipulation tactic some people use, especially the narcissist, to try and cause doubt in the minds of their victims. The way a person gaslights depends on the situation, but the main objective remains the same. They want to reinvent past events to make sure their errors or mistakes stay hidden.

In the example above, Margaret clearly remembers that her mother spanked her and her siblings. This was verified by the conversation she had with her brother, so she knew she hadn't made it up. When her mother noticed how good her granddaughter acted, she knew that Margaret's parenting was working, which showed her choice of spanking wasn't the best discipline method. With this in mind, Margaret's mother wanted to create distance between her and that discipline practice since it has become seen as harmful, ineffective, and unnecessary. She chose to claim she never did it, despite the fact Margaret and her brother remember having to face it as children.

With this example, the gas lighting seems relatively harmless and Margaret could just brush it off. But with narcissistic gas lighting, it becomes extreme, and it can create serious doubt and even cause their victim to start questioning their sanity. This is only one tactic that a narcissist will use to protect their image, not just how they appear in the present, but in the past as well. They have to make sure that they appear correct in every part of their life, so they strive to stay away from being branded for little mistakes even if they took place decades ago. Gas lighting allows them to sweep these mistakes under the rug while also hurting a person's sanity, which to them, means nothing.

Smear Tactic

If you start to notice that people distance themselves from you once you get out of the clutches of the narcissist, they have probably started a smear campaign. While politics typically holds the most popular smear campaigns, narcissists will sometimes use these same strategies. Once you cut ties with a narcissist, they have realized something: you know who they truly are. This means that if you were to start exposing the narcissist for whom they really are, which likely isn't even a part of your plan, then they are going to have to be carefully because their façade may start to crumble. This isn't something that they want to face.

What is a narcissist to do? They will use smear campaigns to stay a step ahead of the game. They use the information they have about you and the relationship you had. They will make sure to talk with mutual friends before you do to clarify the reasons why you two are no longer speaking. This will likely involve tweaking some information to make you out to be the bad guy.

It's important to note that a narcissist is not going to settle for just mentioning a couple of nasty things. They are looking to completely destroy your reputation and credibility. This ensures that you will have a very hard time convincing your friends what you really experienced. You will come off as unreliable, and they keep the friends and their reputation.

If the narcissist chooses to do a smear campaign, it can leave you without anyone to turn to. Some gossip and rumors can be so bad that it harms your job and other relationships. Keep in mind that they never really cared about you to begin with, so don't be surprised if they become somebody unrecognizable and start sharing absolute lies about you and the things you have done.

Abuse by Surrogate

The one thing that a narcissist never runs out of is people. People gravitate towards them for the same reason you did. Unfortunately, if somebody chooses to cross a narcissist, they will find themselves dealing with attacks from the rest of their posse.

This is something that you could refer to as abuse by surrogate, and it will start the moment you upset them. Their need to discourage and shame will hit full force, and they are going to make sure that you feel their unhappiness for what you have done to them. They will also take things a step further and hit where it hurts. This is where other people will step in.

Narcissists, as discussed above, will start to talk to other people in their circle about you. They will convince them that you are the one at fault, and you must be taught a lesson. The interesting thing is that they won't actually say those exact words. It looks more like brainwashing when making other people believe certain lies and encouraging them to act on certain ideas without instruction.

Here's an example: Damito is the middle child. Her sisters are A+ students and they bring home impeccable report cards and get a lot of praise from their teachers. Damito is just an average student. While she may not get the grades her siblings do, she does come home with decent grades. She is by no means failing. One day, though, she fails an exam and her mother loses her mind. She reprimands her, says she's lazy and that she is worried about her future. She says that her performance isn't going to get her anywhere in life, and it upsets her to say that Damito isn't going to achieve what her sisters will.

Damito is sent to her room after being reprimanded in front of the family at dinner. She cries and sulks in her room for the rest of the night. Meanwhile, her sisters are still at the dinner table, and her mother continues to complain. She praises Damito's sisters. The great grades give meaning to the long hours she spends at work to afford their schooling. The children feel happy and loved by their mother's words, and they thank her for all of the effort she has put in to make sure that they can get the best education.

While they are talking, she calls Damito ungrateful, saying she doesn't deserve to get the same opportunities as her sisters because she doesn't appreciate what her mother does. She goes on to tell them that they shouldn't associate with people like Damito because they can be bad influences and cause them to lose sight of the things that are important. Before their conversation comes to an end, she says that she still has to work hard and hopes for the best, even if some of them don't appreciate what she does. The end their conversation and the kids go to bed.

The following day, Damito gets up and heads to the kitchen for breakfast to find that all of the food has been eaten. "You got up late, so you don't get food," her older sister tells her rudely. During the day Damito is showered with the same harsh and negative energy from her sisters who seem to be avoiding her.

This makes her feel ashamed and alone. This causes her to approach her mother and apologize for being ungrateful for all of the work she has done. Her mother "accepts" her daughter's apology, but she stays cold towards her daughter in the next few days, which her sisters mimic. Can you see the problem in this scenario?

First, it's important to see the reason for the aggravation. What did Damito do to get this kind of treatment from her mother and then her sisters? A single failed test. For the majority of us, one bad grade isn't a reason to get this upset. In fact, most parents would let this slide with saying more than, "do better next time."

However, since Damito's mother is a narcissist, she views any type of failure as completely unacceptable. Her children are an extension of her, so if they have any shortcomings, it is completely unforgivable because if reflects badly on her. She made a point of reprimanding Damito in front of her sisters. This shows her anger and imparts shame because everybody else gets to hear and see her receiving this punishment.

Next, once Damito leaves, and her mother continues to talk with her sisters. She starts out by praising them, telling them how proud she is of them being top students. Of course, it's easy to infer that they only perform well because of the pressure from their mother and not because they actually want to do well. By talking to Damito's sisters, she can trick them into feeling the same animosity towards Damito, who didn't even do anything malicious to anybody in the family.

Her sisters and her mother don't have a real reason to be upset with her because the grade she gets doesn't affect any of them. However, since her mother used the tactic of divide and conquer, they feel connected to her and thus become aligned by mimicking how she feels. What happens next? They unknowingly emotionally abuse Damito by giving her the cold shoulder. They distance themselves and treat her like a pariah. This causes Damito to feel the brunt of her "mistake" and she has no choice but to apologize, even though she shouldn't have to.

Abuse by surrogate can be hard to handle because it causes the victim to feel isolated. They start questioning themselves and may even begin to believe their abuser had a good reason to treat them so badly. What's more, they feel the added pressure from the "mob" which complicates their internal battle. If everybody is mad at me, then I must have done something wrong.

What is important to remember here is that just because several people believe something doesn't make it true. When you are at the brunt end of abuse by surrogate, it can cause you to start questioning your validity and integrity, but you stay strong and decide to believe that the truth will help you to be less affected by their abuse and disapproval.

Dealing with Emotional Abuse

If you or your partner find these steps quite difficult, it can be useful to seek professional help. A therapist or counselor can be an impartial guide in following these steps and can provide essential insight that you both missed. They can make sure that the two of you are not seeking to hurt each other, even unintentionally. Although not necessary, a therapist can be a valuable asset in the quest of turning your narcissist partner into an unselfish, loving partner.

It is my sincere hope that you and your partner are both willing to put the work necessary into your relationship to improve it. By following the techniques laid out in this book, you will have the person you love turn into a thoughtful, unselfish partner. But they, too, have to be willing to do the work. Remember, you cannot force someone to change. You can change how you act, but if your partner is not willing to engage in the work laid out in this chapter, there is only so much you can do to improve your relationship. But, working together, you and your partner can accomplish miraculous things. You can get the loving partner you want while and he or she learns to deal with life and relationships more effectively.

Chapter 9
Healing from Narcissistic Abuse

To the people reading this who have survived narcissistic abuse, good for you. Now it is time for the healing to begin. The good news is that there are many approaches you can take to get your life back in order. In applying the various healing techniques, be sure to give yourself time. The abuse did not occur overnight, and neither will your reparations. With these thoughts in mind, here are the recommended healing techniques to revitalize your life after narcissistic abuse.

Meditation

Meditation is a great way to center yourself through active body movement and deep breathing. Healing narcissist abuse brings victims face to face with their source of fear. The memories and images of past abuse that may have been buried will likely be brought to light once you quiet your mind. The intention of this practice is to help you embrace your past experiences, good or bad, while disarming the traumatic effect the bad thoughts have had on you.

Studies have established that meditation can help combat symptoms of PTSD (Cohut, 2019). Meditation reduces the stress hormones by soothing our sympathetic nervous system, which triggers the fight or flight hormones. We have included the following tips to help with peaceful meditation specifically dealing with trauma.

Find a Safe Place to Meditate

After leaving the abuser and ending the toxic relationship, there is a tendency to have flashbacks that trigger panic attacks. The presence of your abuser matters as it reinforces the attacks.

For meditation to be effective, you must feel safe. This feeling of peace must sink into your subconscious so that you relax and feel unencumbered. Find a quiet spot where you are alone, lay out a mat, maybe light some candles. Put on meditation music or "ohm" in a low tone to keep distractions at bay. Breathe, as this is the beginning of healing.

Find Other Ways to Meditate

There are many approaches to mindfulness. In fact, should you develop panic attack or anxiety, doing something, anything, to keep yourself distracted can help. It can be while washing the dishes. With every stroke of the sponge, you can drift into a state of mindfulness. It could be while mowing the lawn, brushing your teeth, etc. All you are to do is focus your thoughts on the task at hand. With this, you are not actively attempting to meditate but to complete your chores.

Be a Witness to Your Flashbacks

It is common for victims of abuse to have physical reactions to any thoughts of their abuse or abuser. With meditation, you can witness your thoughts in a controlled setting rather than reacting to them. While reliving the memories of your abuse, it does not have to paralyze you as it did before. With meditation, you can be a gentle observer of the memories of your abuse. This way, you can strengthen your control which will lead to a significant improvement over time.

Group Therapy for Healing

Group therapy involves the coming together of people in similar situations who have experienced narcissistic abuse. These share their struggles and how they were overcome. This allows victims to come to terms with the fact that they are not alone. Group therapy exposes victims to various approaches through which they can heal. Group therapy offers patience, courage, and strength to heal, recover, and eventually get your mental health in order. It can help tap into the inner strength needed to live a healthy and satisfying life.

A Typical Group Therapy Session

Group therapy is handled by a trained therapist and the sessions consist of six to twelve members all sharing their stories. The idea is for people with similar characteristics (in this case, victims of a narcissist's abuse) to voice their concerns, experiences, and coping strategies in a safe environment. Group therapy works best in combination with meditation and other forms of therapy.

The idea of sharing your nightmares in a room full of strangers might be scary, but it has a wide range of benefits. With the diversity that exists within a group, the victims of narcissistic abuse can develop new and healthy strategies. Hearing others share their tale of abuse can do a lot for your journey.

Types of Group Therapy

Most group therapy occurs in two forms: process-oriented group therapy and psycho-educational group therapy. In the process-oriented group experience, the therapist does not take a major role. They only act as a moderator and encourage members to share. This creates a sense of belonging in each member and a feeling that they are in charge of the session. This is the type of group therapy that best helps victims of narcissistic abuse.

The psycho-educational group experience, on the other hand, puts the therapist in charge. He teaches members healthy and scientifically-tested coping skills to solve various life problems. The therapist is the center of attention here as they play the role of teacher.

Cognitive Behavioral Therapy for Narcissistic Abuse Recovery

Over the years, CBT has proven to be pretty effective in helping trauma victims. The aim is to bring improvement by systematically changing patterns of thoughts, feelings, and behaviors. CBT revolves around the fact that the three are connected and an improvement in one can trigger an improvement in another.

With CBT, patients can learn:
- Helpful coping mechanisms for stress and how to handle trauma
- To interact with their trauma in a new way that does not trigger a negative reaction
- How to develop an objective understanding of their relationship with the narcissist to help revive their sense of control and also develop healthy coping skills.

The therapist helps victims to reconsider their thinking patterns to detect unhelpful patterns. These are the patterns that might have occurred due to continuous exposure to the abuse. For instance, victims might think they are bad people for attracting a narcissist. Unbeknownst to them, narcissists do not take an interest in weak or insignificant people. They prefer to go for strong and powerful people who can soothe their egos, people they can exploit. Victims, however, do not know this. With this therapy, victims begin to see themselves in a new light. The aim is to help bring the traumatic experience to a new light. This way, they get a new perspective about the incidence as well as their ability to cope.

Many times, victims of narcissistic abuse avoid and suppress memories of the abuse or anything that triggers their time with the abuser. CBT can help reduce this by assisting patients in embracing the occurrence in a healthy way. This involves a planned and controlled exposure in a way and at a pace that the patient is comfortable with. This bring control and confidence, rather than resorting to avoidance behaviors.

Yoga for Narcissistic Abuse Healing

Over the years, yoga has grown in popularity as a means of connecting the mind and body. As a mindfulness exercise that uses various breathing and relaxation techniques combined with physical movement, yoga has proven to successfully treat mental health issues as well as trauma from past occurrences.

Continuous exposure to stress and potentially life-threatening situations reconfigures the body into fight-or-flight mode. Even though this is the body's way of saving us from danger, excessive stress raises the cortisol level that we know triggers mental health problems.

Yoga has a soothing effect on all levels of stress in the body. It can calm the body and transport it to a state of tranquility. A common factor with victims of trauma is the inability to adequately process and heal from their experiences. This is why traditional therapy alone is not very helpful.

Introducing Trauma-Sensitive Yoga

Trauma-based yoga stands out in that it directs the body awareness of the present moment to take care of any symptoms arising from abuse or trauma. This emphasizes the internal experiences of the victim who is intending to get in touch with their body at the present moment.

These helpful feelings could be anything from how the cloth hugs their body to the movement of air through their lungs. The aim is exposing how they can take action about their experience. With this yoga practice, students can learn to get in touch with their bodies and minds.

Yoga, in combination with psychotherapy, can help reduce the after effects of trauma and narcissistic abuse while reinforcing positive emotions such as acceptance, compassion, and empowerment.

Self-Hypnosis for Healing

Hypnosis is a way to reach memories that are out of one's consciousness. Self-hypnosis tries to provide a positive restructuring to dissociated traumatic memories. In other words, with self-hypnosis, victims can face their fears and the traumatic time spent with the narcissist. Rather than being hindered by the memory, patients embrace these memories in a new dimension. This is done with the aim of re-moralizing memories like self-protection and at times, pity for the abuser.

With this, victims can access the traumatic memory in a controlled way while viewing them from a broader perspective. There are many forms of self-hypnosis, but we will run through the eye fixation self-hypnosis method in this book. Be sure you are in a quiet room without distractions. Get into a comfortable position and make sure you are well seated without crossing your legs and feet. Your clothes should not be too tight, and we suggest no shoes.

Look up and take a deep breath. Pick a point on the ceiling and direct your gaze, without straining your neck. With your gaze fixed in this position, breathing in deeply, pause, and exhale. Repeat this for sometimes and relax. Close your eyes and feel every tension in your body drift out. Allow Your Body to Relax. Let go of all tension in your body and sit in a relaxed position. Countdown from five and let your body relax deeper with every count.

Direct your attention to your breath, note the rising and falling of your chest. The key is not in trying to relax your body. Rather, it is in allowing your body to relax.

Bring Back Your Consciousness

Count from one to five and open your eyes. Open your eyes at the count of five, stretch your arms and legs

You might not feel as calm as you would want. The key is growing with practice as there is a learning curve.

Using EMDR to Heal Narcissistic Abuse

With Eye Movement Desensitization and Reprocessing (EMDR), victims can unlock past hurtful experiences. It is not a traditional therapy and works best over a few sessions. It has healing effects on the thoughts, feelings, and memories of the past, and in this case, narcissistic abuse.

EMDR is an intense form of therapy in that it seeks to unlock painful memories, associated with the abuser. It is a psychotherapy that helps people heal and recover from the emotional distress of a traumatic event.

Humans generally have either the left or right brain hemisphere dominant. However, EMDR with bilateral stimulation helps activate both sides. Since they both work at the same speed and capacity, there is rapid processing. This reconfiguration makes it easy to identify trauma by highlighting the affected area. Rather than the trauma being stuck, it gets processed in a healthy manner.

Many victims of abuse, specifically narcissistic abuse, react to the memory of the trauma like it just happened. Part of the aim of EMDR is to curtail this. For instance, you remember how your abusive partner yells at you. Nothing you did was good enough which made you sad and angry. The difference now is that even though you remember every detail; you do not feel the anger.

This is what EMDR is trying to achieve. It helps reprocess the memory such that even if you remember how hurtful the experience of the abuse was, you no longer feel the physical manifestation. Not only do you have a renewed approach to these memories, but you also have to let go of the hatred and resentment you had for your partner.

Chapter 10
Dating After Leaving a Narcissist

Getting back control of your life after years of abuse might seem like a difficult thing to do. But with the right guidance and using the right tools, you can effectively regain your control and find happiness again.

Get the Negativity Out of Your System

Like it or not, there is a whole lot of negativity within your system by the time you are parting with a narcissist. This toxicity accumulated as you tried to appease them and in trying to make the relationship work. You tried to understand the narcissist as they took advantage of you more and more. It is now time to let go of all that darkness and allow space for your life to take shape again.

Some of the things you can do to get this negativity out include journaling or sharing your story with a friend, or even engaging a therapist. Talking out the story is so helpful, especially when it is with a listening partner since it helps in organizing your confused thoughts into place. Also, it helps to empower you since you can finally be honest with yourself. You can engage in mind and body exercises such as yoga or dancing that help to discard the toxicity and clears your mind to accommodate positivity.

Compile a List of the Controlling Incidents you Have Experienced

Although this might seem trivial, compiling the experiences of control and abuse helps you realize what you have been through and appreciate your growth - the fact that you will not allow yourself to be in such a situation again. Such remembrance gives you pride in your bravery in leaving and looking forward to a more rewarding life. You appreciate that you can now live as a free person and cannot allow yourself to fall back in the abusive relationship.

Practice Listening to Your Inner Self

Your inner voice is the best tool you will ever have in dealing with any situation. It shows you how best you can do things and it never lies. Even amid great pain and desperation, your inner voice will show you how to find your way out. The major reason why the narcissist was able to manipulate you was that they worked on the external stimulants of your brain, which in turn messed your internal stimulants as argued by Morf, Horvath and Torchetti (2011). They were fulfilling their selfish motives by controlling how your brain responds to things. However, listening to your inner voice will help you review a situation and you can learn when to move ahead, hold back, or reject the things being said to you. It will guide you in your newly acquired life, one in which you are free. Now you understand yourself much better and will never fall for a toxic person again.

Organizing Time and Space

It is good to have a clean and organized space since this allows you enough time to absorb everything that comes your way. When your space is full of clutter, you feel overwhelmed because it registers in your mind that you have a lot to do. Decluttering allows you to organize your space and keep only the things that matter to you. You will find that your brain will respond positively to living in an ordered place. You will feel more settled and you are energized to face every new day. Also, clutter obscures your mind and your thinking. You can establish a good daily routine where your most significant tasks are allocated to the time of the day you tend to be most active.

Connect with Family and Friends

As noted, narcissists usually isolate their victims from their loved ones and friends. They no longer understand you, and they may even think that you hate them. They have judged you countless times because your attitude towards them has changed. Some of them could have tried to tell you that you are not okay in your relationship, but you have always denied their sentiments in an attempt to defend your narcissist partner, who had already conditioned you to support them against all forms of attack. Since you have been dependent on the narcissist for all your social contact needs, you find it difficult to associate with people. The truth is, however, that your loved ones are always eager to reconnect and spend time with you.

Be Patient: Take Your Time

The worst mistake you can commit is to judge yourself and think you are not making fast progress regarding getting out of the pit and forgetting your narcissist. You should not be hard on yourself. Instead, understand that healing takes time to be effective. Also, everyone needs different amounts of time to get over something. Based on the depth of your abuse or length of the toxic relationship, you might need more or less time to heal.

There is no time limit on healing. Remember, your abuser has already separated you from your most precious people and hobbies. They conditioned you into feeling lost and lonely without them. Therefore, healing might take time, and it is upon you to be kind to yourself and patient as you heal. Most importantly, do not jump right into another relationship. This will obscure your thinking and deny you time to heal. Consequently, you will carry the burden right into the next relationship, and it will not be healthy.

Acknowledge What has Been and Forgive Yourself

You might be tempted to beat yourself up for allowing such a toxic person in your life for such a long time. However, true healing and regaining power entails accepting that you have associated yourself with a highly toxic person, who has consciously hurt you. Accept that you have been tricked and abused. Trying to please them and showing them that you understood them denied you the chance to identify the red flags. Also, they used your strengths against you: you were caring, you had a good job, you were highly organized, open to new ideas, and financially stable. You never deserved this, and it was wrong of them to abuse you.

After acknowledging this, know that it was not your fault and forgive yourself. Forgiving yourself is the most important thing you need to do right now. No matter how much time, energy, wellness, and cash you have lost, that is all in the past. You have to forgive yourself and move forward. It does not matter why you stayed for so long, but it does not matter why you were fooled. But it already happened. So, forgive yourself.

Seek to Acquire Knowledge: do Self-Inquiry

It seems so difficult to make sense of the abuse you have been through and what to do after this. For such a long time you have only learned to see the world through the perspective of your abuser. You are now confused and are wondering where to begin. Seek to be knowledgeable about emotional wellness. There are a myriad of articles and online courses you have access to that can help you.

Knowledge is power, and enhancing your power never goes out of fashion.

Shift Your Focus

Because you have been abused for a long period it is easy to find your mind moving back to these thoughts. These are aspects of trauma and cognitive dissonance and are a hindrance to proper recovery. The reason why your mind keeps on pushing you back there is that it wants to comprehend certain things and process related emotions.

You should not entertain these thoughts about the past but capitalize on the present. You may find yourself taking one step forward and two steps backward. Train your mind to be in the present and the future you have chosen to make for yourself. To boost your motivation in this endeavor, you need to resurrect your dreams - and this time let them be magnificent. Remember the dreams and things you wanted for yourself before being drawn to the narcissist; think about how bad you wanted them and boost your desire to achieve them. This is what it means to shift your focus to looking forward and changing your status from that of a victim to a hero in your life. Even though you have been through pain, after healing you may be surprised by the self-loving person - aware, whole, and integrated - you have become.

Chapter 11
Case Study and its Implications

We will now take the case study of a patient called Diana, who visited an individual therapist. This is what was gathered from the therapist's point of view. Diana was raised by a narcissist mother who blamed her for almost everything. The mother would be aggressive to Diana; then, she would tell her poor daughter that it was her fault that her mother treated her that way. Diana grew up with low self-esteem. She became a target for a narcissist partner and fell for him. Finally, she was mistreated, abused, and left in trauma. Luckily she decided to seek help. In the therapist's room, all Diana would do was to blame herself and protect her abuser.

The therapist finally asked, what do you get from blaming yourself and protecting your abuser? What do you get out of protecting your abusive ex and blaming yourself instead?

This was a hard question for Diana, who finally said, I know I made him abuse me. I provoked him. There is something I could have done to make him treat me better. Earlier, he was very nice, and he used to make me feel confident. He always praised me and told me how special I was. I am not ready to accept that he had a personality disorder. There must be a way for me to get him back and fix things the way they were.

The therapist's view

It can be tough for Diana to heal from narcissist abuse. The reason is her history of being forced to believe that it is her mistake to be ill-treated. Her childhood was fractured; she was not appreciated. She fell quickly to the flattery of a narcissist partner. She is stuck and only wants to focus on the good part. We keep on wishing that she get back the excellent experience that first carried her away. Diana blames herself so much, thinking she would have done better if her alleged suitor had remained kind to her.

The reasons why a narcissist becomes abusive are to bring others down and keep them from outshining them. Furthermore, they do it to bring other people under their manipulations. They like being bossy. They feel fulfilled and secure when they know they can order people around them without resistance. A narcissist knows well that they cannot just control grown-up human beings as quickly, so they have well-mastered tactics to achieve it. The narcissist pretends, lies, baits, lures, destroys, and steals the sense of self from their targeted victims. They do their tricks in a much-hidden way such that the victims will not realize that they are succumbing to toxic manipulation.

Diana was taken through all the stages of therapy, and she is now reconciled with reality. The same Diana was told to write another statement of the real things that her mind tells her, but her brain does not want to believe.

What Diana wrote

It is not my fault that he was abusive. There is nothing I could have done to make him treat me better. He has a history of being offensive. He only treats women well in the beginning when he wants to seal the deal. He will eventually mistreat the other woman he is using to hurt me. Other men will find me attractive and love me sincerely .

The Fate of a Narcissist

It is very devastating to see a narcissist get away with their hurtful deeds. You have been traumatized, mistreated, abused, threatened, and deprived of your happiness, and then the narcissist abuser is basking in the sunshine, enjoying his new life to the fullest as if you had never existed. This makes you think that the order of things in the universe has no room for serving justice, even for a religious person, who finds their faith distorted and starts thinking there is no compassionate creator who watches over good people. In your mind, many unanswered questions can be tossed and turned; you are wondering why the wrong people get rewarded while the competent people get hurt and destroyed.

Let's try to answer some questions: Do narcissists enjoy the rest of their lives without karma serving them their just desert? Do they continue destroying people and getting away with it? The answer is no. No matter how long it takes, everyone ends up with what they deserve. This benevolent universe grants us divine compensation for what we have lost and immense tribulation to the abusers. We do not need to do anything to make this happen; it just happens naturally.

Getting the bigger picture of the fate of a narcissist can be the key to recovery. People often ask themselves, when is the narcissist going to pay for all the horrifying things they took me through? The truth is that they pay for it every second of their lives. You may not directly understand this, for maybe you see them succeeding in life with big cars, big houses, and new lovers who appears to outdo you while harbor your pain and loneliness, with no single penny to your name!

True happiness comes from within and not without. The most valuable riches one can possess are the riches of being your true self. This is one thing the narcissist lacks. Understanding this, you can start to connect, get passionate, and create wealth from other beings. Make sure what you do is heartfelt and sincere and whatever you attain brings peace and satisfaction. If only you release that distorted perception instilled in you by the narcissist, fulfilling success is on its way. This is opposed to the narcissist who doesn't experience their true self and has no permanent connections to anything. They may appear ambitious, for there are always fantasizing about new heights of success. But in reality, this is a perversion that costs them a lot. A narcissist does not find permanent happiness, whatever is exciting to them now will be lifeless and unworthy sooner or later.

Their need for a new supply of emotional and physical things is insatiable. Eventually, they get devastated. The universal system gives more than being to a person, and the narcissist ends up being more frustrated, and feeling more pain and emptiness than other people think. The narcissist is an accurate representation of a disconnect. They have a disconnect even with their cautiousness. They cannot experience love and any other life force. This makes it challenging to come out of their devastation. They further fall into drug abuse and other self-destruction activities.

Nevertheless, as a person who wants to heal and move on with life, it is good to focus not on where the narcissist will end up but on yourself. It is good to know that they will pay for their misdeeds. As for you, concentrate on yourself. Instead of stalking them to find out how much karma has done, focus your precocious energy on how to heal with life, get your true self back, and stand on your feet again.

A narcissist hides their true self. So, even if they are going through hell, they make people believe they are succeeding. If you base your happiness in seeing them suffer, you might not be pleased in the long run. Base your happiness on yourself, who you are, who you are becoming, and the good things that are on their way.

Narcissists' victims fight these dangerous narcissists who plan to ruin the lives of their innocent partners. You will successfully come out of stress and disappointments. The effect of many a narcissist has left several love partners ending their lives under messy conditions. Narcissists have significant effects on relationships and not to their benefit. the victims need to change their patterns with these narcissists' abusers. This can only be possible when they escape the narcissist's abuse. You will be able to distinguish yourself from people with this terrible disorder.

According to a variety of studies, narcissism happens mostly in men. The individual has a false sense of self-admiration while seeking excess respect from other people, both known and unknown to them. If not treated in a timely fashion, the condition can translate into more profound side effects. It escalates as far as affecting all people around the person. People affected by the disorder are not capable of tapping into other people's emotional world or showing any form of empathy.

A narcissist quickly flies off the handle at the slightest disagreement. They believe they are the "mighty superhuman" who is to be worshiped and never criticized. Propping up these delusions takes some work; hence, their dysfunctional attitude and behavior tend to stick around. They protect their imagination with defensiveness and rage at the slightest provocation.

Overall, these people are not capable of handling criticism and always disregard how other people feel. To date, this behavior remains a mystery, although a professional can diagnose the condition and treat it with therapy. Having knowledge of the number of people living with a narcissistic disorder offers some comprehension of the situation at hand. Knowledge improves outcomes for people living with this mental condition. The clinical life prevalence of narcissistic personality disorder is at 2-16%, and 1% for the general population. According to studies conducted by Twenge and Campbell 10 years ago, NPD has doubled. Studies also show that 1 in 16 people in the population are living with this condition.

Dealing with a narcissistic personally takes a toll on individuals, both psychologically and emotionally. First encounters with people who display this behavior see them as charmers until you start interacting with them. Be it at work, in a relationship, or as parents with children, you tend to feel some form of suffocation, or struggle with pain and loneliness.

In the end, narcissistic personality disorder has both physiological and physical effects. The physiological effects of NPD can have an immense impact on mental health. Some of them include zero interpersonal skills, hypersensitivity to criticism or insults, increased feelings of anxiety or depression, and low self-esteem. On the other hand, the physical effects of NPD come from various unhealthy behavior such as an arrogant attitude or behavior, over aggressiveness, the increased risk of abusing alcohol or drugs, and suicidal tendencies.

Since it is not a well-known mental disorder, people live with this condition despite the dire consequences. Seeking treatment is essential for the well-being of the person and their loved ones.

Conclusion

Narcissistic relationships are often complicated; many people who fall prey to narcissists never realize that they were involved in a relationship with a narcissist. There's a lot of information on the internet that explains how narcissism develops, but in order to understand it, it has to be experienced or observed firsthand.

Many of the signs mentioned in this book might not be visible from the outside but can lead to an unhealthy relationship if left unattended. It is also important that we become aware when someone we love is being abused because it can save their lives. Once again, dealing with a narcissist is not an easy task as they are great manipulators. They might start off as a soulmate and then reveal their true colors later on. While many narcissists will promise to love you forever, many will lead you on and leave you when they see an opportunity to get what they want somewhere else. Many people who are in relationships with narcissists tend to be idealistic and very naïve to the dangers of such relationships.

It is important to understand that love can be a very complicated concept, especially in the narcissistic world where everyone is very selfish. We are told from day one as an adult that we are our own person and we don't need anyone else's approval, but we should always strive for our own goals, ideals, ambitions, etc. However, when it comes to love, we might find it hard to understand the concept. Don't let your life become a complete waste by giving in to the narcissist's demands.

www.ingramcontent.com/pod-product-compliance
Lightning Source LLC
Chambersburg PA
CBHW071519080526
44588CB00011B/1494